PINBOY

PINBOY

GEORGE BOWERING

a memoir

Cormorant Books

The publisher gratefully acknowledges the support of the Canada Council
for the Arts and the Ontario Arts Council for its publishing program.
We acknowledge the financial support of the Government of Canada
through the Canada Book Fund (CBF) for our publishing activities,
and the Government of Ontario through the Ontario Media Development
Corporation, an agency of the Ontario Ministry of Culture,
and the Ontario Book Publishing Tax Credit Program.

LIBRARY AND ARCHIVES CANADA CATALOGUING IN PUBLICATION

Bowering, George, 1935–
Pinboy : a memoir / George Bowering.

ISBN 978-1-77086-401-6 (PBK.)

1. Bowering, George, 1935– —Childhood and youth.
2. Authors, Canadian (English) — 20th century — Biography.
3. Oliver (B.C.) — Biography. I. Title.

PS8503.O875Z472 2012   C811'.54   C2010-904413-4

Cover art and design: angeljohnguerra.com
Interior text design: Tannice Goddard, Soul Oasis Networking
Printer: Trigraphik LBF

Printed and bound in Canada.

The interior of this book is printed on 30% post-consumer waste recycled paper.

CORMORANT BOOKS INC.
10 ST. MARY STREET, SUITE 615, TORONTO, ONTARIO, M4Y 1P9
www.cormorantbooks.com

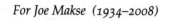

For Joe Makse (1934–2008)

I am no lover of pompous title, but only desire that my name
may be recorded in a line or two, which shall briefly express my name,
my virginity, the years of my reign, the reformation of religion under it,
and my preservation of peace.

— ELIZABETH I

PINBOY

CHAPTER 1

WHEN RITCHIE SCHNEIDER stood eight feet behind the release line with a black ball held under his chin, I was truly afraid. It was as hot as hell in that pit behind the five pins on their black circles, and thank God we were allowed to take our shirts off. I was fifteen years old and covered with sweat — my skinny torso with no hair on its chest, spindly arms, a big adam's apple, my dark hair slick with sweat. We were backed by a half-inch sheet of black rubber that kept the heat in, and we were on the second floor. It was the only bowling alley I had ever heard of that was on a second floor. That was one of the stupidest ideas in a valley that was full of stupid ideas. The owner, Bruce Dunlop, lived in back below it.

Outside, the temperature had been nudging a hundred all summer, and was still in the eighties in September. It was probably a hundred and forty in the pinsetter's pit. There was always a silent understanding around our house that I was a lazy boy, but setting those pins at the high speed required by the bowling alley was really hard work. It made a boy ache in bed the way only old folks were supposed to ache.

When Ritchie Schneider's crowd was bowling, I thought I could hear hard death coming, hard side-of-the-cranium death. Every kid knew there was a spot on your temple, that if anything hit it hard, you'd be gone. Your parents wouldn't have time to get there.

Ritchie Schneider rushed the line filled with fury, his hand with the black ball in it pointed straight to the ceiling behind him, and when he let it go the ball did not touch the hardwood lane till it was half way to me. He usually demolished that triangle of schmoos with those black rubber waistbands added for greater bounce, then there was a clatter of wooden pins smashing each other on their way through the air, some of them whopping the rubber sheet a quarter of a second later, some taking a terrible skip up off the wood and past my ear.

Every time Ritchie Schneider let a ball go with that anger of his, I wanted to scoot out of there. But if I ran and there was a pin left standing, Ritchie would shout about the delay. He was ready to spare. I don't know whether he looked for the fear in my body, but I would not be surprised. My Sunday job was keeping score at the Oliver baseball park, and Ritchie was never going to forgive me for two bad things I had done. One was to indicate in my scorebook, and then in the weekly Oliver *Chronicle*, that he had made an error at third base on a grounder hit to his left, and the other was to aver that a ball he had hit between the Penticton shortstop's legs was an error rather than a single.

You could go deaf back there in the pit if all the bowlers hurled the ball as fast as Ritchie Schneider did, and a lot of them pretty nearly did.

You caught hell if you put the pin imperfectly on its black circle, but you had to do it fast, too. They screamed at you if they could see you moving when they were getting ready to roll. Sweat poured down your arms, and into the hands you were trying to be perfect with. Every time someone bowled ten frames you got ten cents. That was a penny for every time you set up five pins and rolled back the balls.

I preferred the business of keeping score and writing baseball and basketball news. For that I got fifteen cents an inch. I would cut my stories out of the *Chronicle*, and then once a month or so take them down to the newspaper office and cash them in.

Your life in a small town half way through the twentieth century was measured in cents.

But the bowling alley wasn't all fear and Ritchie Schneider. Sometimes I would spend a line's worth of pennies on a bottle of pop from the machine. I did Coke and Pepsi no good. I was the kind of kid that must, they knew, have existed — I favoured grape pop or the fizzy green stuff made right up the road in Penticton, Mac's lemon-lime.

I took small sips to make it last, while I jumped back and forth between my two lanes. Once in a while the skinny guy in the next two lanes would sneak out behind the rubber for a half a cigarette, and I would have to try to keep up with four lanes. When Ritchie Schneider smashed the pins, some of them would come to rest in the pit behind another lane. The skinny guy was about thirty, I guess, and wore a baseball cap backwards, the way the tough guys did back in those days.

I liked it better when I was setting for the teachers' league. It was a little embarrassing, I guess, because most of the teachers knew me as the science teacher's son. I didn't make eye contact. Especially when it was my father's turn to bowl.

My father was a good all around athlete, but he always had his own way of doing things. I, on the other hand, was an inferior athlete, because whenever I got into a situation such as shooting baskets, I would always strive for style, which meant trying to wind up in the posture I would see in the pictures in my sports magazines. In five-pin bowling my father had a pretty respect-able average, one of the best in the teachers' league, but I didn't like to watch when he approached the job. He would stand way back by the chairs, the ball in both hands under his chin. Then he would walk purposively and quickly to the line, bend, and release the ball with a minimum of body torque.

If it had been me, I would have held the finishing pose, right leg back in the air, foot pointing somewhere high to my left, right arm still high above my head. Not Dad. He would be turned around and walking back, the little smile on his lips letting you know that he knew he had a strike.

At least I didn't have to worry about pins flying toward my temples. In fact there weren't any killer bowlers in that league. The closest was Bob Shannon, an avuncular man with a poker in his spine, who had worn a moustache and driven an important staff car in the Second World War, and now taught English history at Southern Okanagan High School. He gave firm handshakes and kept his blue blazer buttons done up. At the bowling alley, he thought of the triangles of white pins as the Maginot Line.

The worst bowler in the league was the red-headed woman who taught art. In the classroom she liked to perch on the corner of the teacher's desk, and the guys in my class at least, guys like Art Fraser and John Jalovec, were forever dropping the pencils they were supposed to be sketching with, and reaching down to the floor to get them. I could never figure this out: was she completely unaware that fifteen-year-old boys took every chance there was to look up an adult woman's skirt, or did she enjoy the thought of the excitement we felt along with our jollity?

So here in the pit of the Oliver Bowling Lanes for the teachers' league, I was daydreaming. Or actually, I was trying to remem-ber what island was closest to Anguilla. The Lesser Antilles were hard as the dickens to keep straight. This was long before I ever heard a Caribbean guy speak, and there had never been a movie set in the Caribbean at the Oliver Theatre, as far as I could remember. So the Islands were basically a map, and pictures of palm trees. For some reason I had a sense that there were no palm trees on Anguilla. Then it was her time to bowl again, the art teacher.

This would be around the fifth frame, so I treated her the opposite of the way I treated old Ritchie. She generally rolled all three balls into the gutter, and if there wasn't some peculiar Newtonian law at work, they might have stopped half way to me. So I would step down from my perch and wait to catch the ball in my hands as it finally dropped off my end of the gutter.

Art Fraser and John Jalovec never had it so good. This almost made being a pinsetter worthwhile. First she came as slowly as my dad did to the foul line, but she did it bent way down, and I could see a vast percentage of her breasts. Even though the foul line was by the rules sixty feet from where I was also bent over, those breasts were, well, you likely know from your own experience. There were two things we boys usually called them — tits or cans. The first time I read about them as "breasts" I thought it was kind of strange, because I always had thought of "breast" as singular — what we have as the top part of our chest — but then I also thought "breasts" was sexy as hell, pretty near dirty, as we said, a lot more so than "tits."

The red-headed art teacher, whenever she was bowling, would wear the same outfit. On top was a kind of jersey thing, I guess you'd say, somewhere between a thin sweater and a very loose tee shirt, always white. Below that was a black and white and red plaid skirt, the kind that would swoosh if you sashayed, so that when I finally took my eyes off her tits, there was her skirt swooshing, and I saw her legs and then some, I mean way up to the white that matched her jersey. Aw, I was just getting the first hint of a notion that a teenaged boy could desire an old woman in her twenties.

But I had to pretend I wasn't looking — not particularly looking. It would not be too bad if she saw me looking, skinny hopeless jerk down in the dark end of the hardwood lane, but I couldn't have the other teachers seeing me look, not Bob Shannon, not Bill McLeod, not my dad.

But when I went to bed that night I would grab myself and think about the art teacher. Taking for given, of course, that there was an impossible thing not even thought out, not halfway imagined, because I was a high school kid with intact virginity, and this teacher, she was from somewhere, the coast, maybe, where adults you didn't know came from.

Still, she must have seen me looking. I never once imagined that she might go to bed and grab herself. I didn't know about that.

St. Martin, St. Maarten. I think that was the island.

⸪

I CAN'T EVEN remember the art teacher's name, though I remember her legs. They were maybe just a little thicker than average, something I have always perversely liked. They were more inviting of a caring hand on their surface. I am a little out of touch with that teenage Bowering's mind, so I don't know how far it was allowed to go in thinking about those round legs. I just kept grabbing fivepins, two in either hand, and slamming them onto the little black circles called their spots. But her legs were just a little past average. Not as far past as those I saw more often below the skirts and shorts of Miss Verge.

Miss Verge was the Business and Home Economics teacher and the girls' counselor at school, which even then struck me as odd, but there you go. I mean she was single, and in fact would remain single till her fifty-first year, which was a good long time after the events I am more or less telling about.

Miss Verge bowled a ball that was just a little faster than the art teacher's, but it stayed out of the gutter quite a bit longer. I hopped down into the pit when her third ball was on its way, and of course had the experience of looking up her skirt at just that moment when her arm was high and her knee was bent. Her legs were wider than those of the art teacher, and her calves stuck out farther, and there were two reasons for this. Miss Verge was short and somewhat wide, and she was an athlete.

Now if I went into a long description of Miss Verge's body, it would just, the description that is, run up against any reader's ingrained prejudices about human bodies. If you just will not think kindly about a body that is rather short, a bit wide, and well-muscled, what is the use of my proposing all the possible details here? Now I am not a big fan of short and wide myself, but short and wide and athletic is a lot different from short and well, just fat.

However you feel about it, I have to warn you that this story I am writing is going to be about Miss Monica Verge. My first plan was to tell the story of my whole life, but I have seen what happened to a friend of mine when he started that. He has already gone half a million words, and is still talking about elementary school. Forget it. So I decided to tell about a moment in my adolescence, and I mean adolescence, when I was trying to live an ordinary kid's life while trying to keep four female human beings happy.

Another one of them was my mother, so I'd be out of luck there. The best I could do was not to bring her to the edge of tears. Well, I had never seen her there, so I supposed, as a kid will, that that was at least okay.

One was a girl from the other side of the tracks, and in this little account her name will be Jeanette MacArthur. More about her later. She is the one I didn't understand, or rather, when it came to her, I did not understand what the hell I was doing.

And the last one was Wendy Love. I was, as is to be expected of a boy who reads a lot of books and listens to a lot of romantic radio, in love with love. I am really sorry, but that was her name, or at least an accurate translation of it, and we are stuck with it.

Wendy did not have perfect Eaton's catalogue legs, either. Her legs were just a bit too straight, and her ankles were just a little thick, the way I like them. It strikes me now that I don't remember at all what Jeanette MacArthur's legs were like, but that's all right. I am talking about Wendy Love's body. Do you know what I mean by "just a bit too straight"? Put it this way: when girls are around six years old just about all of them have these stick legs, and some of them still have them when they are sixteen. It doesn't mean that you don't want to get your hands on them. It's just that you can see that a girl with legs like that has been managing for some time to walk around on imperfection — seeing whether she can make do and be ordinary.

Popular or otherwise stupid sentiment or composition have it that these girls should become librarians and schoolteachers. Nurses, on the other hand, have to have the kind of legs you want to see when they are leaning way over to adjust something on the other side of the hospital bed.

But I was in love with Wendy. And seeing that I seem to be assessing or at least remembering body parts here, I might as well get the next items over with. Wendy did not have her teenage girl's share of breasts. (I think that she might have been the first person to use this word in conversation with me and made me blush.) Fifty years later my right hand and I remember how good it was to hold one of her little breasts.

I have another friend who has always preferred women with

small breasts, whereas the US entertainment industry has always tried to teach us that we men like football and fast cars and big tits. I have always wondered about my friend — whether he prefers small breasts because he wants to pretend that his woman is a girl. Nothing wrong with that, don't get me wrong.

Wendy was born in England, but she had a nice tint to her skin. Her little breasts would not have had brassieres on them if this had all happened a few decades later, but in the early fifties a girl had to wear a bra, and sometimes a girdle, and often a crinoline. When I got Wendy's little bra loose or off, I saw even in the light of an Okanagan moon that her breast was just faintly lighter than the rest of her skin, and that it was a hillock.

I am not satisfied with that description, but it came to me.

She had other ways of being unlike the girls in the magazines. Her eyebrows, for example, were almost non-existent. They were lighter than her light brown hair, and they were sparse. Her nose had a bump halfway up, she had a crooked canine tooth, and she had a freckle or mole on the left side of her neck. But she had green eyes. I would propose marriage to a tapir with green eyes.

About her English accent I felt conflicted and sentimental. You have to understand that my home town was not all that much older than I was. It was younger than my parents were. After the First World War, the government, whoever they were, decided to turn the south Okanagan into an Eden for army veterans. The Valley had been a desert where the Okanagan Indians had enjoyed living. Then it became ranching country, and then mining country. Now it is wine country, but when I was a kid it was orchard country, and a lot of the orchards were owned by people with English accents, because when the government decided to offer dirt-cheap land to veterans they did not distinguish between Canadian veterans and what we called Limeys.

So there was the setup for my Capulet and whatever conflict. I had not in those years yet become an anti-USAmerican, and I was not a rabid Canadian nationalist, but I really did not like those Limey bastards. In the Valley the Limeys were cliquish. They all went to their Anglican Church and its spinoffs. They were in the same clubs and so on. They had picnics in each other's orchards. They grabbed all the good jobs, and the ones who had been privates in the British army now strutted around my home town, wearing blazers and those slanted-stripe ties that indicate that you were some pip pip officer or country gentleman.

Limey bastards, I always said.

But I was in love with a Limey bastard's daughter. All right, he was not as bad as some of them. He was a little guy who had been a gunnery officer in the navy, but he did not strut around in a blazer. He had also been the lightweight boxing champion of the Royal Navy. It never entered my mind to engage in any disagreement with him or to take advantage of his elder daughter. And Wendy's mother was a very nice woman who made her own mayonnaise, and did her best in a farmhouse that had no plaster on the interior walls yet. She is a woman in her nineties now. When I saw her two summers ago she complained that I was supposed to have become her son-in-law.

I just naturally presumed that Wendy was a virgin like me, but there was a faint rumour lying around somewhere that she had been hot with this big handsome guy in her class, a guy from Osoyoos. He died under a snowslide in the mountains west of there. Wendy was supposed to be hot in grief.

This is something I haven't talked to anyone about for over a half century. He was a year or more likely two ahead of me in school, some kind of athletic hero I didn't know, and why would I? Anyway, he was a patterned-sweater-wearing skier, and a climber and all that. Around that time or a bit earlier, the best young swimmer in Oliver drowned in the river, fell off a chair he was sitting on in the water; and the best young skater in Oliver fell through the ice on Tuc-el-Nuit Lake and was pulled under the thicker ice by a current and disappeared. I felt safe because I wasn't the best at anything physical in that town. But there was this story.

There had been a big windy snow storm in the mountains I have never climbed, on the west side of the valley between Oliver and Osoyoos. It was not until this moment that I noticed I never climbed up and back into those mountains. I wonder whether this was why: the guy in question, tall, fit, went, as they say, missing, and crews went out looking for him, a grade twelve boy or man, who could take care of himself, people thought. Were there others who did get out, did get found? Why don't I remember more of this?

Well, the story we heard from each other was that he had eventually been found, released by the snow, and it had been a long time. He had chewed off the ends of his fingers.

Did this really happen? Was it a story whose edge had been caught by some boy from some uncle reading a newspaper story out loud? Was that it, something like that?

But such stories do fall away, don't they? My classmate Tibor Palley died in the hospital, and the story we heard was that he said over and over, "I love you, Jesus." A few years later no one ever mentioned Tibor Palley. The kids a couple of grades younger than us probably didn't hear his name much.

SO I JUST figured I would ignore all that stuff. When I finally got the nerve to touch her chest she did not make the customary teenage girl move, the one where they shove your hand away but not too hard. Wendy taught me how to kiss. "Loosen your lips," she said. "I am not your granny."

I sang popular songs, and she hardly ever told me when I failed to hit the note:

They try to tell us we're too young
Too young to really be in love
They say that love's a word
A word we've only heard
And can't begin to know the meaning of

I felt bad about finishing a sentence with a preposition. I was always running across this problem — do you sing bad grammar or do you change it and sing an awkward song?

Bobby McGee and I?

Julio and I, down by the schoolyard?

I can't remember whether Wendy ever put her hand down my pants. I don't think so. Maybe girls you were in love with didn't know how to do that back then. Some women, maybe. Not girls.

CHAPTER 2

SETTING PINS AND writing about basketball weren't the only jobs I had. In the summer that year I worked at the Mac and Fitz packing house. According to the union or the government or somebody, you were supposed to be sixteen years old before you could work there. I was a pretty tall fifteen, though I was pretty skinny, and tough guys called me baby face. I forget exactly what I made there, but I think it was about seventy cents an hour.

At Mac and Fitz, peaches would be coming by on a conveyor belt, and women with rags on their heads sat on both sides of the conveyor belt, and took hold of peaches. The first women the peaches got to were just looking for culls. If a peach was too small or not coloured enough, these women would take them off the belt and stick them in boxes. The best of these culls would be packed off to the cannery or the juice plant, where they would go through another sorting, and then the really bad ones would be put in boxes and carried up the hill road to a place where the truck could back up to the edge of a little soft cliff, and two guys in the back of the truck would dump these peaches over the cliff, where they eventually formed a big hill, sort of yellow in the bright sun. Next spring there would be a big mound of peach pits, and growing out of this mound would be a few baby peach trees.

The peaches that passed inspection would go to the women toward the end of the conveyor belt. They would grab the good big colourful peaches, wrap them in a piece of paper faster than you could see them, and fill up peach crates. You had to have just the right number of women with fast hands, and just the right speed of conveyor belt, or you would wind up with peaches all over the oiled wood floor.

This is where fifteen-year-old George came in. My tool was a handtruck. It was designed to stack five apple boxes, but it was recommended that you stack six and don't have an accident. I can't remember how many peach crates you could stack — probably about ten. If you were working the culls, you would always find a pile of boxes full of them, and you would get the lip of the truck under a stack, stomp on the grabber, tilt this five-hundred-pound pile back toward you, find just the right rhythm, and wheel them away toward the loading bay for culls.

Or you would find a stack of good crates and haul them toward cold storage, where they would form part of a huge stash of perfect peaches that would eventually get rolled onto a refrigerated truck and taken away to some grocery chain, who knew? When you got back to the conveyor belt there were two or three stacks waiting for you and whoever was working with you. It was really hard to keep up — a killer to keep up. The women on their chairs felt sorry for me. They said a boy shouldn't have to go so fast all the time.

At lunch I gobbled my jam sandwich, huge bites, and then some older guys taught me how to play poker. Not how to play it well enough to win.

But I didn't blow all my earnings and I never signed an IOU.

About four years later something like this would happen in the air force, where I was a feckless worker. But I never lost my whole two weeks' pay on payday night there either, the way some people I counted among my friends did.

I sweated a lot, but you don't take your shirt off if you have to wheel peaches into cold storage. My shirt was soaking wet down the back, and that felt bad enough in that cold summer's room. One of the women told me, finally, that I should bring an extra shirt to work. I could leave one to dry in the sun outside while I was soaking the other. This woman was just like a mom. In fact, nearly all the women on the conveyor belt were moms of kids my age or younger. But some of them were young Doukhobor women. In the Valley in those days, the hottest thing we boys could think of was the Doukhobor girls. They had a kind of glistening to their skin, something that told us that the mystery of their background was something beyond just German or Hungarian. It was something that was hotter and damper and darker and more yearning than anything a regular Valley boy would know, he with his grandparents from England, where they wear ties to work in the vegetable fields.

When you were bragging to your friends about the fucking and so on that you never really got, and it was the treefruit season, and people were sweating anyway, you usually told a story of you and a slightly older Doukhobor girl named Polly in the high grass where the mowers could not reach.

I was the kind of boy who believed most of these stories when they were told by the other guys, the less studious ones — the ones who did not read books and magazines, and therefore had to use their time in pursuits such as car repair and poontang.

There was tall grass at the base of each tree in the orchards because the mowers that were driven up and down between the rows were not allowed too close to the trees, for fear that the

bark might be scraped off. Once in a while you would be walking through the orchard, moving sprinkler pipes, for example,
and in a sudden rush of noise that made your heart nudge your
throat, a brilliant pheasant would leave his hiding place in the
tall grass and fly a little and hop and fly and walk away.

The first time I actually removed Wendy's entire little bra with
the little safety pin in it, we were in her family's orchard. Aw,
there was her naked trunk in the sunlight. I could run my hands
up and down her sides. I could nuzzle in that space between her
breasts. I got scared of being caught by her short father with the
fists, or anyone, really, and gave her back her bra pretty soon.
This was the first time I had seen nipples sticking out.

Not counting my mother. No one can remember back that far.

But most of my experience of orchards involved work. In
September every year the teachers and principal at school would
tell us that if we were doing well in our classes, and had had
a good spring as far as academics went, we could skip school
and go and make money picking apples for a week or two. I was
the boy who believed my classmates' sexual adventure yarns. I
believed the teachers and principals. Probably some of those car
repair boys knew that the orchardists were desperate for pickers
in the sudden rush of the season, and this was the only way the
crop could be saved.

I knew how to pick apples. I knew how to get to the top step
of a sixteen-foot ladder and get those winesaps into the bag in
front of me. It was a canvas bag reinforced with galvanized tin,
and every kid knew how to tie it, how to open it and gently drop
a bagful into a box that became a boxful, and maybe another fifteen cents. A good picker could do a hundred boxes a day. On
my best days I topped twenty.

Once in a while I saw Polly on her ladder, reaching up in the
sunlight, reaching for a big Red Delicious, and I could see up and

in her short sleeve, and it was hard to tell for sure, but she might not have had a bra on.

I started working in orchards when I was twelve. I knew how to strip suckers, which I would do while the orchard owner was pruning. I knew how to thin apples, stack boxes, prop apple trees, pick cherries, pick apricots, pick peaches, pick pears, pick prunes, and pick all the varieties of apples. I knew how to change sprinklers, load trailers, and even drive tractor a little.

Sometimes I worked in the orchard from eight in the morning until it was getting a little dark. Sometimes I worked only until the end of the afternoon because I had to set pins that night.

One job I was not too crazy about was at the swimming pool. In the South Okanagan all the waterways are loaded with green slime, some kind of sleazy biological goo that found its way into the lakes, rivers, irrigation canal — and the village swimming pool. Once a week the pool would be drained, and I would get into it with my big bristly broom and pitchfork and clean it, pushing as much stuff as possible into the drain at the deep end, and pitchforking the rest of it out, later filling my wheelbarrow and hauling the thickest green slime to a pile that turned brown after two days in the sun, the same Okanagan desert sun that would turn pollywogs to jelly in a couple hours after you dumped out your jar. I never did that, but someone always did.

Sometimes I would find things in the pool: coins, keys, lipsticks, extra hard turds. It was always as hot as hell when I was brooming down inside that concrete cube, and the sun that measured ninety degrees outside on the grass of the baseball park, must have been a hundred and thirty inside that box. Once I did it with no hat on and wound up in the hospital with sun stroke. I have used that as an excuse for all kinds of things ever since.

My mother, who was sometimes one of the conveyor belt moms at a different packing house, thought it was swell for me to have that swimming pool job. She thought I was saving money for college.

All these jobs were supposed to be for college savings. They would have been, too, with some change put aside for baseball magazines and western novels, twenty-five cents each from the corner store across from the movie theatre. Oh yes, and twenty-five cents for the movie theatre.

I never took Jeanette MacArthur to the movie theatre. Jeanette and I were unofficial. She was a fairly good-looking girl with long legs, but what she looked like had nothing to do with it, at least as far as I was concerned.

How am I going to introduce the subject? This part is harder than the Wendy part for sure, and even harder than the Miss Verge part.

Jeanette lived on the other side of the tracks, literally. Down on what we called Sawmill Road. It probably has a number now, a number with five digits that no one can remember. That is what happens when the province decides it should pay attention to little places that have grown up without a digital sense of order. Digital these days has very little to do with fingers.

Oh, I am avoiding the subject.

Way down on the wrong side of the tracks. The only good thing about that part of town along the river was the preponderance of weeping willows. Every yard had a weeping willow or two in it, along with some really tall grass and a few discarded truck tires.

Okay, the earliest detailed memory I have of Jeanette is her uncharacteristic outburst in grade six. I forget what the class was, but our teacher mentioned that the average head of a household, and she explained that this means the father, earns two hundred dollars a month. Jeanette, who was usually quiet, shouted, "My father doesn't make two hundred dollars a month!"

I had no idea how much my father made, probably about two hundred dollars a month. And we still weren't allowed to flush after just a pee, or have both butter and jam on a slice of toast.

Jeanette did not wear absolutely crappy clothes, but she wore nearly the same clothes every day, and they were all home-made. I gloried in the shirts my mother made for me — she let me pick out any pattern I wanted from the Eaton's Catalogue, and of course I picked out the wildest ones offered. But Jeanette's clothes had stripes, and they were faded.

⌐━⌐

WHEN I WASN'T working or hiking in the hills or playing my home-made baseball game, I followed people. I would get behind a guy coming out of the bank and go wherever he went the rest of the afternoon. If he went home I would wait outside his house, peeking through windows, sitting in a hiding place and reading my book, say *Silvertip* by Max Brand.

Four years after her outburst I followed Jeanette MacArthur. When she walked home after school she didn't walk with any-one. Usually, when I followed someone who was walking with someone else, I didn't have to be extra careful, because they would be talking with each other and paying less attention to whatever was in front of them or behind them. And she had a long, long walk down to Sawmill Road and about a mile south of town. The kids there were less likely to have bicycles than were the kids up in town, so most of them had to walk. Maybe they should have had a school bus, but I'll bet that the school district planners didn't even think about Sawmill Road.

I had my technique for following, or tailing as we sleuths put it, but it was harder to fade into the environment on Sawmill Road than it would have been uptown, where you could just nose your face into the Rexall, where the latest issue of *Sport Life* might be. But she didn't notice me, never looked behind her, just walked the most ordinary of walks till she got to her place, and turned and walked in there, quiet as deep illness, pretty as an arm pain.

So I took up my post, and when some kid from grade seven came by I was a bottle collector, but that was not very well thought out. On Sawmill Road a lot of bottles might get thrown into the ditch from passing cars, but they would not stay there for more than three hours. I loitered, and this was the most challenging tail job I had ever started.

Her house was all on one floor, a grey bungalow with curling tar shingles on the roof, flakes of paint along the window edges, and a few wooden steps to the front door. Right behind it was a lot of grass about ten feet high, and behind that was the river. There was no garage and there was no car, and there were no tires in the yard. A willow wept over one end of the roof. A thick dark rope hung from a branch, one knot in it. Weeping willows weren't for swings, I thought, but that was the kind of tree they had down there in the hollow. We didn't call it the hollow, but romantic people from the big city probably would have.

I saw her through the window, throw her books on some kind of couch with a brown blanket over it. Then she went into the back, so I did too, into the grass, which was more like it if you were sleuthing and didn't want grade sevens looking at you funny. She wasn't anywhere, but then she was in the kitchen. She reached down, and then she stood up, an apple in her hand.

Here in the Valley an apple is no treat. The cheapest person I ever saw was the woman on the block north us, who gave me an apple in my Halloween bag. Everyone in town had boxes of apples. They were the next thing to free, and sometimes they were free.

"I'm hungry," I would often say.

"Have an apple," said my father, who was brought up in the Valley.

Jeanette ate the apple, staring out a glass part of the kitchen window. About half the panes were made of cardboard. She stared, and I thought she must have seen me, but her eyes looked as if she was not seeing anything. People look like that when they are planning their escapes to Tahiti.

She disappeared into the front room, and I was just getting ready to scoot around there when she came back with her books. She sat down on a wooden chair and opened a book and put her chin on her hand and her elbow on the table and read about New France, if she was keeping up in class. I had to pee like crazy, and for a while I upbraided myself for even thinking of peeing in Jeanette's back yard, but then even though I was in the high grass, I went almost down to the river and peed.

When I came back she was peeling a potato. I watched. She did not touch another item of food. She cut the potato into pieces and put them into a pot of water. I hung out in the grass, wishing that I had a folding canvas camp chair. I wondered about snakes. The only snakes to worry about were rattlers, but I could not imagine rattlers down in the wetlands by the river. Rattlers were supposed to be basking in the sun next to a rock and some sagebrush.

At five o'clock she ate the potato.

I decided that I would follow her at noon the next day, instead of going home for lunch.

I DON'T KNOW whether you know this, but De Quincy, in *Affliction of Childhood,* says that we adults don't have enough memory of childhood to revisit it, much as we would like to, that all we can do is to visualize it. You know what that leads to. But in a "note to the reader" at the end of his three-volume memoir of his childhood in the Bronx, Jerome Charyn says: "Although this memoir was inspired by the experiences of my childhood, certain characters, places, and incidents portrayed in the book are the product of imaginative re-creation and these re-creations are not intended to portray actual characters, places, or events." Notice that he calls "actual" people "characters." Very interesting, as they used to say. "Imaginative re-creation," eh? Don't you get the notion that this guy is trying to keep you in the dark when it comes to whether the stuff really happened?

Well, I have to tell you that I don't have any power of imagination. I am not re-creating any of this stuff. I think it all happened. If I remember what a folded five-dollar note that had been in my mother's purse smelled like when I was at the store buying her some cigarettes, I might not be able to describe the smell, but it happened, and you know it did because something like that happened to you. Now whether my mother would hand me a whole fiver to get her some cigs is another question. But I am not one of those question people.

I think that goopy kid George Delsing was or maybe still is. There were a lot of reasons not to want that bozo around. He was a smart-ass, for one, and he may even have been kind of smart, but no one likes a guy that is a smart-ass a hundred percent of the time. It was bad enough that we had the same first name and the last three letters of our last names. He was a year ahead of me in school, which means that he was in Wendy's grade. I even saw them talking to one another from time to time. I wanted to pop him one right on the nose. I think a lot of guys, and maybe even some of the teachers, wanted to do that. I am just mentioning him because he is now some kind of writer, from what I have heard. Okay, I have read parts of a few of his books. He's still a smart-ass. One of those question people.

⌒

WHAT WAS I supposed to do when Wendy let me take all her clothes off in my mother's cabin?

I don't want to tell about that quite yet. I don't even want to think about it. She was lying on the couch, white and smooth and fragrant.

Here is what did not happen. I was hiking with my dog in the hills back of the umbrella tree, looking for a pond I had found up there a couple of years ago. There are not a lot of ponds up in the hills of our desert valley, but way back then, when there was one, there were no houses circling it. My pond was about the size of a baseball infield, and not much deeper than a standing teenager at its deepest part. It was in the middle of range land, so sometimes you might see some cow plops around the edge, and during the second time I had been there I saw a cow standing in the water.

On three sides it was rocky, with a little rock cliff on one side, over which water dripped into the shade. On the fourth side there were a few reeds and some smooth black stuff that was halfway between fine sand and mud. In my head there was an ongoing expedition, and there this pond was called Edgerock. I should have been a real estate advertising guy.

On the afternoon in question I walked out of a little clump of red pines, and there was my pond, sparkling except in the shaded part. Standing in the pond, white and thin in the sunlight, water up to her kneecaps, was Wendy. On a dry and weather-greyed windfall tree were her skirt, shirt, and other things. I went straight to them.

"Go away," she suggested.

"I will give you back your clothes," I said, "after —"

"Just go away, George."

She had her arms over her chest, hands on opposite shoulders.

"— after you come out of the water and dance."

"For one thing, there is no music, Idiot, and —"

I began to sing.

> They tried to tell us we're too young
> Too young to really be in love —

Did she dance? Did we embrace? Did someone else, someone on a horse, discover us and call us by our names?

It never happened. That is not how I fell in love with Wendy. I never saw her entire nakedness until that afternoon in my mother's cabin. I was a mountain-climbing boy and all I saw at the pond were hoofprints from two or three cows. Being the boy I was, I began to pretend that I was a sheriff on the trail of rustlers.

But I never saw a naked girl in a pond. I don't have the imagination to make one up. I was a sheriff without a horse, a boy with an erection in his corduroy pants, staring at an infield of water.

❧

ONCE I READ an essay by that Delsing idiot. He was going on about some newfangled theory of writing. He said that all the action is in the language. It's all about language. Language is the only reliable thing. Sure. Give us that kind of crud, and us readers are left without the pleasure of imagining the scene, say some boys throwing apples at each other in an orchard. Or clumps of couch grass, get ahold of them by the long dry stems, and whirl them and then let them fly. Whack a guy with a clump of exploding dirt, right in the middle of the chest.

❧

MISS VERGE LIVED in an apartment above The Food Basket. That was the name of a grocery store that defied the powerful chain Overwaitea. Its site had been where the chain Red & White store had been. I had no political conscience in those days, so I did not prefer it to the Overwaitea with its big green teakettle sign hanging over the sidewalk. But I do remember that Willy and I set up one of our cryptic photographs there. They hadn't finished putting up the sign yet, and we spotted our chance. Willy stood in front of the store, and I squatted in front of him and snapped an image of my pal and "The Foo." That was a term used in Smokey Stover, one of the greatest comic strips of all time. That's where I learned via a stitched sign on Smokey's firehall wall that "The Foo is mightier than the sword." Etc.

I took another famous cryptic photo in front of The Food Basket. Its subject was a man holding up copies of *Awake* magazine, which was funny only because the man seemed to be asleep, standing with eyes closed, back of his head on the glass.

I was noodling down the main street, a copy of *Raiders of the Rimrock* by Luke Short, let's say, in my hand, when out of The Food Basket came Miss Verge, pushing the glass door with her shoulder, and struggling with a big box of groceries. I saw that she favoured Bran Flakes, as I did. Without thinking, I grabbed the door and held it open while she shuffled sideways to the sidewalk.

"Could you —?"

The box began to escape her grip. I threw my drugstore Bantam Books paperback on top of her groceries and grabbed the box just in time. The fingers of my right hand were holding the fingers of her left hand to the cardboard. Phew. She struggled loose and said, "Thank you."

I carried the box of groceries up the long flight of stairs to her apartment, a strong boy. She climbed in front of me, keys in her right hand. There was just a weak lightbulb near the top, and these were steep steps. Miss Verge was wearing heels and a tweed skirt, a little tight in back. I saw the general shape of her behind, and I could see the backs of her legs in their sheer brown stockings, those muscular legs that I usually saw from in front. The difference was that now I could look and look without turning my head. I stumbled once, and a grapefruit fell out. I trapped it with my left foot, thank goodness, because it would have been embarrassing to go all the way back down the stairs for a grapefruit. And then try to guess whether she would ever eat it, given the circumstances.

At the top I was puffing just a little. The box of groceries weighed less than half of what a box of apples weighed, but the steps were steep and long. It was dark inside her apartment except for a thin rectangle of sunlight on a hardwood floor. Then it was lighter, because Miss Verge opened the drapes all the way.

"Oh," she said, noticing that I was just standing there holding a box, "in here," and she led the way into her small kitchen.

My dad was the chemistry teacher. I had been in a lot of teachers' homes, but this was the first time I had been in Miss Verge's place. In fact I had never been inside an apartment before. My mother played badminton with Miss Verge, but I don't remember her being at our place. Not often, anyway.

I set the box on the table, right on top of an open *Scribner's* magazine. I felt air going down the back of my neck.

"Can I help you put stuff away?" I asked.

What? I thought: what?

"That's okay, George. You have been a big help already."

Schoolteacher, I was thinking. Schoolteacher.

"You're welcome." My reputation as a quick thinker and rapid-fire wit would have taken a hit if any of my schoolmates had been there then.

"Would you like a cup of tea? I'm going to make myself some tea."

"No thanks, I'd better get going."

"There are Mum's Cookies in the grocery box."

"Ah, no. Maybe next time."

"Next time?"

"Uh," I said, and that is the level to which my repartee had fallen. "Uh, I mean if you ever need me to carry your stuff upstairs."

"That would be very sweet of you," she said, and then we were walking to the front door.

"Thank you again, George. I always thought you were a good Samaritan."

And as I turned to go out the door, I felt her hand on my side, just below my ribs, just above my hip!

CHAPTER 4

USUALLY AT LUNCH I walked downhill on a dirt road to our little home, where I would make myself a bowl of Campbell's vegetable soup and a jam sandwich on white, polished off with a slurp out of the kitchen tap. Then I would read the paper. We got the Vancouver *Sun* the day after it was printed, so if I was looking for the score of the Bruins-Maple Leafs game, I would get it the day after the night after it was played. Years later, when I moved to the coast, I had a hard time getting used to the idea that I was reading the scores from last night's game.

Sometimes I would skip lunch and go with a bunch of boys to the pool hall back of the Orchard Cafe. We were never supposed to go to a pool hall. That's where people wore tattoos, expressed themselves with crude vocabulary, and maybe even turned their backs and sipped at a mickey of rye. You could go in there if you were sixteen years old, and anyone who was fourteen years old was judged to be close enough.

There were Indians in the pool hall. Manuel Louie, the chief, had a big pot belly, which he would rest on the cushion while he made the sweetest lightest movements of his cue and ran the table. He was the king with a turkey feather in his cowboy hat. He ruled the room and made romance for every boy with any imagination. Until Windy Bone came along, that is. Windy Bone was an old Indian who looked younger than Randolph Scott, and he had a habit of stroking the cue ball before it had stopped moving, and in that room usually filled with the loud clack of ivory, he would drop every colour of ball into whatever pocket was nearby, and if you had your back turned, you wouldn't hear the contact.

There was a cafeteria in the basement of our school, and I can almost just barely remember going there a few times to have whatever they were making, probably meat loaf and mashed potatoes, glop out of a long ladle. Whenever I try to remember our cafeteria, I get it mixed up with the cafeteria in *Archie* comics, thinking about that frizzy-haired woman with the squint who glops something on Jughead's plate.

I think that more kids from Osoyoos and Okanagan Falls and out in the orchards brought their lunch in lunchpails or paper bags than went to the cafeteria. They might go to the caf for a glass of chocolate milk. But moms in the South Okanagan in those days were more likely to make sandwiches or make their kids make sandwiches than try to find cafeteria money. Sometimes I took my lunch, if I wanted to do something at noon hour, such as practice the tuba with Will on the front steps of the auditorium. I hated it when I would unwrap the wax paper from the chocolate cake, and the icing would come off and you had to lick it off the wax paper. Imagine, hating your lunch.

But it was no use looking for Jeanette MacArthur in the cafeteria. I decided to check around outside, to see whether she might be having a sandwich with someone down by the irrigation ditch or up by the skid trail or back of the schoolbus garage. I spent most of lunch hour walking from place to place. I did find Leo

Smith and a girl whose name I can't remember, both with their shirts off, in the back seat of Leo's dad's car parked beside the road that separated the school grounds from the nearest orchard. I gave Leo a big toothy smile, and he gave me a hand gesture that I was accustomed to.

I did a quick check inside the school, even looking into the metalwork shop. I thought about the girls' washroom, but a certain episode of two years ago had taught me to stay outside that place. But now noon hour, which in our school's peculiar system was forty minutes long, was over, and I had to go and sit in Social Studies for a while, learning yet again about Cardinal Richelieu. I wanted to get into a time machine and go back and poop on his rug.

All right, my sleuthing technique was hardly tested at all. I had a million ideas and the right mixture of patience and concentration to apply them. The following day the boys in my class had Phys-Ed, and we were supposed to be in the gym, tumbling and climbing knotted ropes and that sort of thing. No teacher ever took attendance at Phys-Ed. They might notice that a certain boy wasn't there, and send the vice-president after the slacker. But I decided to take a chance. I went into the strip room with everyone else, taking off my regular clothes and putting on my gym strip. I hated this too, being particularly shy about my bare prick. Some boys could walk around with their pricks hanging in plain view. I even had trouble pissing in a urinal if there was anyone else in the room.

When all the other guys in their shorts and tees and sneaks ran out onto the gym floor, I dithered over a shoelace. Then when everyone else was gone, I changed back into my regular duds and carried my gym stuff back to my locker. It was a little risky being out there in the hall without a note from anyone, but I, the secret detective of Southern Okanagan High, had sleuthing to do.

When the loud noon buzzer went off, and half a second later the door of Jeanette's classroom banged open, I was lurking behind a folded up firehose, ready to tail, to trail, to haunt like a personal ghost. Katie Eisenhut saw me and smiled the nicest smile, Katie in her white and dark blue saddle oxfords. Sylvia, the red-head I had been in love with last year came by and gave me a smile and then took it back. They were coming out of their Typing class. I could see Miss Verge gathering up stray paper while talking animatedly with some future secretaries.

And Jeanette. There she went, very very quietly, north along the brown hall, in the opposite direction from the cafeteria stairs, books held against her chest, head down so her eyes would not meet any rude boy or friendly teacher. I followed at a distance, saying in my head "doo dee doo dee doo," innocent as a fly in the cream.

Our school was shaped like a big letter E. Jeanette was walking along the bottom of the E, and when she got to the end, she would have to go right to the door that led toward downtown, or straight ahead into the gym, or left to the almost enclosed court-yard whose surface in those days was mainly gravel. She opened the crashbar of these doors and went through as quietly as she could. I stood there looking through the round window till she had crunched her way over the gravel some, then quiet as a moose made my way out into the blast of Okanagan springtime sun.

I diddled with some gravel at my toes, watching her step out of the heat of the sun into the tropical heat of the greenhouse.

Now I couldn't very well follow her inside, not if I was still gumshoeing rather than, say, trysting. So I followed as well as I could from outside. Some of the glass was streaked with white goo of some sort. Sometimes big hanging plants obscured the view in either direction, I hoped. You weren't supposed to go into the greenhouse. It was part of the agriculture program. We had four streams in our high school. I was in 10A, which stood for Academic. There were some kids in 10B. I don't know what B stood for. It wasn't business, because 10C meant Commercial. And then 10D stood for Agricultural. There were no girls in 10D or 11D or 12D. The general notion was that D secretly stood for Dumb. I tried not to think so. There were quite a few members of the basketball team in 11D and 12D. And I was the basketball scribe. You see what I mean.

Jeanette had been in 9B, but now she was in 10A. I should have asked her what the B stood for. I think someone once suggested that it stood for General. That wasn't much help. Maybe it just meant *not* A or C or D.

What was she doing in the greenhouse? Later in the spring some of the greenhouse windows would be open, to let the heat out, but this day they were all closed. It was probably as hot as the hobs of hell in there, whatever they were.

Last time I had peeped at Jeanette MacArthur through a window she had been eating an apple. Now she was eating something — she was eating a tomato. They were growing tomatoes in Agriculture. That's one of the reasons we were not supposed to go in there. Another had to do with the proximity of gravel and larger stones to the glass panes. Boys, the staff obviously thought, will be boys. But here was a girl, eating a tomato. She was a fruit and vegetable fancier. Was she hiding out, or was she a salad freak? There had to be a reason for breaking the school law. There were a lot of school laws I had broken, but I had never been inside the greenhouse.

It must have been hot in there. She must have been sweating. I hunkered down in a piece of shade. I wanted to see the sweat on her skin when she came out. I wanted to keep an eye out, in case a teacher or a monitor came by to check out the greenhouse. Why didn't they keep a lock on the door?

Should I go in and talk to her? I think I knew already why she was eating a tomato that wasn't quite ripe in the school property. I didn't want to embarrass her. When she came out I did not rush up to her. I followed some more. She walked past the top part of the E and across the road and down the path between the last two houses on the edge of town and up the skid trail to the first boulder, a littler higher than the nearest roof. I think I was out of sight. I was behind an old weathered wooden fence, in the shade, getting a good look at her more or less, a rogue apple tree with its first pink blossoms between us.

She took another tomato out of somewhere and began to eat it. It wasn't quite ripe either, but she leaned her chin forward so that no seeds or juice would dribble on her pale yellow blouse. I hadn't eaten anything since my bedtime bowl of Bran Flakes the night before, but I was not hungry. I was a detective boy thirsting for info.

She wasn't wearing a watch, and neither was I, so she must have guessed when it was time to head back in and beat the loud buzzer. I sidled up to her about the time she reached the bottom of the skid trail. I just walked beside her and didn't say anything. We had never walked anywhere side by side. She wasn't in the choir and she wasn't in the band, so I didn't normally see her outside of the classes we had together — English, Social Studies and French.

I thought she wouldn't say a word. She walked pretty fast and I walked just fast enough to keep up, which was about half as fast as I usually walked. But as we were crunching across the gravel she said something, though she did not turn her face in any direction but straight ahead.

"What were you doing in my yard?" she asked, and then just plain ran to the door and ducked inside.

I had a habit of talking out loud when there was no one else around. It made up for my habit of not talking much when there *were* people around, unless I had just thought of something really witty to say, especially if I had a feeling that most of the people around me wouldn't get it — I mean, what is a sense of humour for if not to help you with your little superiority complex?

"Hoo boy," I said out loud, "a master detective."

*W*ENDY LOVE WAS in the choir and she was in the band. Well, she was just plain one of the most musical people around our school. It was part of her Englishness, I always thought. I figured the English were just better prepared than we were about music, about serious music, I mean. Most of them did not have a clue, I figured, about the hit parade. I bought *Hit Parader* and the other magazine just like it, for the lyrics to all the radio songs, though I knew them anyway from the radio playing quietly in my room at night.

But in all the orchards owned by Englishmen around Oliver, English people would get together around pianos and sing old songs in four-part harmony. There would be tea and cigarettes, and little kids lying on their stomachs on the floor, elbows on the rug, *Boy's Own Annual* or *The Beano* spread beneath their gaze, Grandma not standing but sitting in her chair, head back on a doily, teacup in saucer in her hands, once in a while pouring a little out on the saucer and slurping it, smiling while all the younger English people sing a song from 1910.

Once in a while I would be there in the Loves's unfinished

front room, afraid to hit the wrong note while Wendy's hands lunged at the keys and her sister and parents sang loud and without fear. I was in the school choir, but there I was a voice among thirty. I could mouth the words, and I often did. Gar McKinley, the choir instructor, would come around and cock an ear, and then you had to produce. I hoped for the best. I could make up for it in the band, blowing loud on my double B-flat tuba.

Wendy knew that for all my knowledge of titles and lyrics, I didn't have perfect pitch. But I knew all the hit parade songs and I knew all the classics. I said that "Stardust" was our song, the prettiest standard around, followed in second place by "Deep Purple," followed in third place by "Body and Soul." Don't worry, I knew important things too — I kind of knew where Dar es Salaam was and I knew the valence of Sodium. But I also knew Rogers Hornsby's lifetime batting average.

"What is the use, if I may ask, of knowing Roger somebody's batting average," my almost agreeable mother would ask.

"Rogers. Not Roger. Rogers."

"Okay, Georges," and she did not pronounce this the French way, "what is the use of knowing some ballplayer's batting average?"

"When," I rejoined, my facial expression meant to indicate that she had walked right into a trap of my devising, "When I am the sports editor and head baseball writer of the St. Louis *Post-Dispatch*, such details will stand me in good stead."

"Set the table for supper," was her reply.

But boy, it was hard to be satisfied with myself when I was in the Loves's front room or sitting with Wendy in the Anglican church. I felt a real pull, sensing the easy fellowship of all these people with their annoying but comforting accents, while trying to remember that I was a rebellious Canadian boy who hated to see some foreigner on the two-cent stamp.

It was all over the country. Every time you turned on the CBC you heard an English voice. It was authority. Oliver had a really good theatre group, but almost all the plays they put on were British, and most of the actors had English accents, natural English accents. The magazines that came from back east somewhere, *New Liberty* or *Maclean's*, nearly always had someone from the British Royal Family on the cover. Whenever you went anywhere to get something from the government, the person you were allowed to talk with had an English accent.

Thank goodness not all the teachers at SOHS had British accents. There were a few with fake Brit accents, but they were easy to dismiss. Whenever they got going, I made sure that I exaggerated my American accent. But when it came to the stuff you learned, a lot of that was English. Year after year we heard about the difficulties between the Yorks and the Lancasters, I think they were. We probably heard the same stuff they were hearing in Kenya and Jamaica. Pip pip, and all that.

There were Okanagan Indian people living on the wide bench just above the Valley along the east side. We never learned a thing about them. They weren't the Lancasters. I never saw Manuel Louie holding any White Rose. My buddy Willy could do a perfect snotty English accent. He would say, "Oh, I say, RAwther," in an English accent, and I would slug him one. I lived a rich fantasy life.

But I never whacked Wendy Love. I never went into my anti-imperialism rant with her around. I still spelled things the USAmerican way and I made sure that I pronounced words the USAmerican way, but I never made fun of her for the way she wrote or said things. I knew I was a young genius, though not a person who was so gauche as to get good marks in school. But no matter how rebellious and heroic, I still felt deep inside my bones that just because she was from England she was smarter than I was, and my only hope was to steer the conversation to subjects that she knew nothing about, such as Max Brand or Ty Cobb, but just one look down her long English nose and I was aware that these subjects were not going to be there when the Final Trump sounded over the abyss.

"Why do you work so hard to make people think you're an idiot?" she would ask me from time to time.

"Who are these people?" I would ask, putting a look on my face that signified my *hauteur*.

"You really do have a superiority complex."

"No, simple."

"Yes, you are, sometimes."

"No," I said, refusing to negotiate. "Simple, not complex."

"I said com*plex*, not com*plex*."

"Yes, but you say to*maw*to."

That worked. We started singing the song. She forgave me my incorrect notes, and I prompted her with the lyrics half way through.

"You understand that I am simply obeying the instructions of Ira Gershwin's lyrics when I say let's call the whole thing off," I said.

"You had me thinking there for a minute, Ears."

"In fact, let's call the whole thing Fred," I continued.

"If I want to hear bad jokes, I will listen to George Formby," she said, putting her fingers into her ears.

"Who is George Formby?"

I knew who George Formby was. He was an Englishman who was apparently very funny in England. But not over here. I had to pretend I had never heard of him.

"You don't know who Winnie the Pooh is," she said, exaggerating her London west side accent, I suppose.

"Winnie the who?"

⚓

THAT DID IT. A few nights later I was her little kid, curled up in her lap while she read me the first chapter of *Winnie the Pooh*. I would never admit it to her, of course, but I liked it. Somewhere in me was a little core, a pit, a stone, a seed of an English boy. And somehow I remembered a bear I had never heard of. My grandfather had come to Canada as an orphan teenager, working like a pale indentured labourer. He never told me about Winnie the Pooh. He had a nice big bookshelf in his front room in Summerland and then in Penticton, before he came to live with us in Oliver. He had the *Apocrypha*, I remember that, and I read about Judith and the old guys glomming her bare bum, and he had Bulldog Drummond, and other things British and leatherette. But no Winnie. Of course he left England before Winnie got there, so I was left with that prairie girl that goes to Oz.

"How did a bear get the name Winnie?"

"I don't really know. I have never given it any thought. Perhaps it is short for Winston," she said. The moonlight was in her face. We were on the verandah, and the moonlight was coming through the screen. So were a few mosquitoes who had found the bad hole in the corner.

"If this were a Canadian book, I would guess that it was short for Winnipeg."

"No."

"Keystone City," I said.

"Well, Winnie is a good British bear," she said.

"Do you have a lot of bears in England?"

"Well, stuffed —"

"A lot of kangaroos, kangas, roos?"

"Toys. The characters in this book are based on the toys that the real Christopher Robin had."

"Kangaroos from Australia. Tigger from India. Small maybe from Africa somewhere. Why couldn't Winnie be from Canada? The colonies demand equal representation," I said, thinking that I was just prattling.

"I know who you are," she said, raising her British nose a little. "You are Tigger, and you are not from India, so your whole theory is down the drain."

"Tigger? I think of myself as still and meditative."

"Tigger," she said, removing my hand from her little breast.

You know what it's like in high school, or rather if you are as old as I am you remember what it *was* like. When I was very young my mother gave me the information that while boys' shirt buttons were on the right and the buttonholes on the left, it was the other way around with girls' shirts. So I knew which side of Sylvia McIntosh I wanted to sit on when it came to classroom desks. Every once in a while she would lean a certain way and a quick eye could see between the buttons, and there it was, her brassiere! Then at night, while you were supposed to be in bed reading three chapters of *Canyon Passage* by Ernest Haycox, you could picture using your boy fingers to undo, say, one of those buttons.

One thing I knew was that girls did not imagine using their girl fingers to undo our buttons, or zippers. This was the main rule of human society, or at least that is what I told my pal Willy — guys are always trying to get girls to give it to them, and girls were always trying to stop guys from getting it. This would even carry on into marriage, with some accommodations.

Wendy would usually let my hand rest on her little breast for just a short while before picking it up and putting it aside. Sometimes I would kiss her, in an attempt to distract her from this action, but despite my hopes, she would remove my hand and then breathe into my ear — a mixed message if I ever received one.

Every once in a while she would feign astonishment at some

of my colonial ways. "One does not," she would inform me, "say aigs and laigs." The product of poultry is called an egg. The lower limb is called a leg. Both these words rhyme with "beg."

"With what?"

"Beg."

"Oh please, please," I would say.

That is when I would get a playful little Imperial slap on the face. But you know, now I wonder whether she was feigning that astonishment about my crude Canadian ways.

I think that maybe it wasn't just my boyish good looks that persuaded her to be my girlfriend. I suppose my half-hidden intelligence had something to do with it. But the crowd that she was brought up in, those sons and daughters of Limeys, were inheritors of the self-regard that made their parents want to pretend that they were all country squires, that the mud and chicken shit on their rubber boots were markers of condescendence. I mean to say that those were human beings trying to be as conventional as they could.

Once in a while Wendy would ask me the same question that was often asked by adults, related to me or not, and the question would include the word "mature." This was a popular word in the fifties. The president of the United States was bald. So was the prime minister of Canada. So was the principal of our elementary school. There was a lot of maturity going around.

But I think that this English girl with the straight light brown hair and the home-made sweater set was interested in being with me because there was something in me that observed the conventional people with disdain, a disdain that itself hinted at sophistication or at least the promise of maturity. Maybe that was in her heart. But then I would spend a day walking backward, and she would be challenged by a contest between disappointment and pride.

Her father's orchard was three miles south of town, maybe ten acres between the highway and the irrigation ditch. On the other side of the ditch the hillside was straight out of a novel by E.E. Halleran. You walked along with your eyes looking at the ground in front of you because you did not want to startle a rattlesnake, so you saw sagebrush, tumbleweeds piled up against a fence, low clusters of cactus, drying cow pies and horse buns, some flowers you had always liked but did not know the names of. Higher up the hills you could see the fans of shale and other rocks that had slid down so long ago that thin grey moss was forming on them. Running down a shale slide was the kind of fun your mother did not want to hear about. With a hillside sliding under you, you had to step a big step and do it before you knew where your foot was going to land.

Years later, if you were a poet, you would use this activity as an analogy for writing poems.

Other times you would be running downhill, around the skid trail, say, and with your right boot you would pick up a few cactuses, and then with your next step you would drive those cactus needles into the inside bump of your left ankle. You would do that several times a year, and the activity would never become an analogy for any kind of writing in later life.

I never went to these brown hillsides with Wendy. I would take my little dog Dinky with me sometimes, and in earlier years I had often hiked them with my pal Willy. But when I was fifteen I was usually up there alone. When I was fifteen I spent most of my time inside my head, and that was an enjoyable place to be if you were alone on a dry hillside over the Valley.

I had been alone three years earlier when I found a dead horse, already halfway reduced to leather, lots of old dry horse buns around him, a rope tying his head to a fence post. A breeze took most of the smell away. I stayed for about an hour. Okay, this is some sort of education, I told myself. I still believed in God. I did not go over in my mind a list of reasons why that horse died tied up off the path up in the hills. I only figured that something crazed had to have happened. And I did not tell anyone about what I had found. If it had been a human being I would have told people.

Speaking of education, I should mention that although she was a grade ahead of me in school, Wendy was a year younger than I, just about the same age as Willy. Oh, and speaking of Willy, he was a good singer. In choir I would lean toward him to pick up the right note and try to copy it.

"Tigger," she called me.

She was not the last to do so. Imagine that! And there I was up in the hills by myself so much, deep in lonely and quiet thought.

CHAPTER 6

*M*Y MOM AND dad played badminton every Wednesday night at the high school gym. In a small town like Oliver the high school was in use every night and every weekend. The actors' club rehearsed and presented plays in the school auditorium. The quilters' club and the glee club used the facilities, as they were always called. A men's basketball league and a women's basketball league used the gym a couple of nights, and volleyball players used it another. Sometimes my parents went up to the gym on tumbling night or whatever they called it, those people leaping over a horse or hanging off rings.

Sometimes I would go to badminton night, and if the regulars were short a doubles player I would get in. I never did learn to play tennis, but I loved whacking birds. This was the time when the plastic bird, or shuttlecock, to use its fancy English name, was introduced, another of those new things that let you know that the world was getting more tawdry, like the light cardboard that was replacing the tin as packaging for a "flat fifty" of cigarettes. I liked the old bird made of feathers. I loved the way it turned in flight so that the head was there for you to whack. Our family being the way it was, we played with highly mutilated birds, but once in a while my father would finger a new one out of the tube and we would try to hit it without ever making a rim shot.

Everyone wore white. My father had white slacks and a short-sleeved white shirt over his white sleeveless underwear top. I had a white shirt with the sleeves rolled up, and a huge pair of white shorts that had appeared as if by magic when it became clear that I was going to be a badminton boy. I shut completely out of my mind any speculation as to what rump these large shorts had covered before they covered my skinny ass. If the world is truly going to the dogs, people probably don't have to wear white on the small town badminton court any more.

My mother wore a white pleated skirt that came down a few inches below her knees. She was proud of her legs, partly because my father was always praising them, and in her innocent mountain girl way she would frisk about, intent on playing the game as well as she could, paying no attention at all to the flipping of her skirt. I agreed with my father about her legs, though for myself I still preferred Wendy's, that were a little too straight, or, say, Jean Jensen's, that were just a tad thick at the ankle.

Miss Verge wore a white pleated skirt, too, along with white ankle socks and white sneakers and a white blouse with buttons in the back, and a white ribbon in her hair, which was pulled back off her face. She was a really good badminton player, and when she and my mother played doubles they hardly ever lost.

Miss Verge spent her weekdays teaching girls how to type, to sew aprons and bake pies, and she counselled them when they had the simple teenage problems we had back in those days. But on badminton night she was an athlete with a strong desire to prevail. She was short but she covered the territory, and had thin tall women of any age gasping for breath by the end of a game. She herself would be glistening, fine perspiration on her forearms and at the edge of her hair. Unlike the good sport she had just defeated in a friendly match, she would be only slightly winded, just enough for me to catch a glimpse of her breasts rising and falling.

Okay, here is what it was like. In proportion to herself, Monica Verge was just perfect. She was shorter than most, and she had more meat on her than most of the women in the gym, but she was in proportion to herself. Do you get what I'm saying? She was not fat and she was not droopy. Her muscles were what you would expect from an athlete. Everything was just a little wider than the model, as if making up for her lack of height. If you had been able to grab her head and hold down her feet and pull upward on her head, you would end up with a body anyone would like to have a feel of.

I wanted to be good at badminton, but as in just about everything else, I wanted to *look* good. My favourite shot was an overhand smash, but the kind in which I would reach over above my left shoulder with the racquet in my right hand and lean into it. In fact sometimes when I could have just got under the bird I would stay to the right and lean over for this spectacular shot. If my father was on the court he might offer one of the quiet cryptic remarks he was so good at.

One time I tried my big important shot and the bird rocketted off into the indoor sky. Miss Verge, perspiring sweetly somehow, took the opportunity to give me some advice after the match. While other people were dashing about on both sides of the nets, she gestured at me and led me to a free area under one of the basketball nets.

The sound of strings whacking shuttlecocks filled the gym.

I was sweating from my singles match, which I had lost but during which I had got off a few photogenic moves. My shirt was stuck to my back and it was beginning to get a little cool. I wished I had a towel, but here I was, trying to make my instructor happy. She wanted to show me how to make that overhead smash without twisting myself into a photographer's dream. She leaned her racquet against the wall, and took hold of my wrists. I had to bend my knees a bit because I was closing in on six feet tall and she was not that much over five.

"Okay," she said. "Just try to relax here, and let me move your arms."

"Okay."

She lifted my left wrist until my arm was out to the side. Then she lifted the other and pulled it back. I tilted the racquet to the left.

"No," she said quietly. "That's going to get you one spectacular winner and a dozen outs."

She moved the racquet so that it was actually leaning just a bit to the right, up there behind my right shoulder.

Then she wanted to move my left leg forward.

She touched the back of my thigh lightly and pushed gently. I moved my leg forward.

"Good," she said. "Now hold it. Imagine a nice high bird coming your way."

And as she let go of me her breast touched the side of my body. It slid on my side just above my waist.

She went and picked up her racquet, bending at the waist. I was afraid that she would look and see the front of my shorts.

"I think," she said, "that you have some natural talent. You just need someone to help you with the fundamentals of the game."

What, I wondered, did she mean? Was I just imagining things? She's a schoolteacher, after all, I told myself. How old is she anyway?

When my mother asked me whether I wanted to hit a few

while we were waiting for a game with the Shannons, what could I do with my shorts like this? I said no, I just want to catch my wind. She looked upward, where the custodian of good sense might abide.

Actually my pants were like that a lot in school. Boys learn, I think, how to walk bent over a bit at the waist. If only I had learned to be boastful, to practice a little exhibitionism. But no, I was embarrassed a lot, especially on any occasion when one was expected to stand up. I would have to linger while the classroom emptied at the end of English period. I hated to be called upon to stand up and explain something. I'd know every detail of the Treaty of Utrecht, but I would have to mumble that I hadn't read about it yet. I masturbated just about every night, so you would think that I would get some relief. But no, and it was not just about the girls in the hall. I would just have to think about the art teacher hiking her bum up on her desk, and I would have a pole a cat could climb.

Of course I wished like crazy that Wendy would just touch it. She wouldn't have to grasp it or move it. Just touch it. But this was early in the fifties. She was a girl who wore a sweater with a dickie and a pencil skirt that came down to her straight calves. It was so tight that she had to turn sideways and pull it up just a tad in order to get up the steps of the school bus when the band was going to play out of town. And then there were her white bobby socks and saddle shoes. Don't get me started. So no, she would fool me once in a while, put her hand on my thigh briefly, at a movie, say, but then she would take it away. Did she want to? Should I take her hand and move it for her? I had no one to advise me. I had no older brother — or sister! — and any of the guys at school, well, you can guess what they would say.

So I would think of Wendy and put my own hand on it. If she only knew what she was doing in my imagination!

Wendy wasn't the only schoolgirl I thought of while I was pulling my wire. I went through just about everyone in my home room class, even Doreen Schmeck, who carried around both a lot of pounds and more than her share of dirt. I would imagine standing her in the tub and covering her with soapsuds, and washing her vigorously, while she wept tears whose cause was ambiguous at the least, and then I would ejaculate onto the magazine I kept open for that purpose. When I saw Doreen walking down the hall at school, her blouse imperfectly tucked into her grey skirt, I never felt a buzz.

But I never pounded my pudding to an image of Jeanette MacArthur. Her face or her body would flit into my head, and I would shake it away. I didn't want to. Was I thinking of Doreen and Jeanette as victims? It couldn't be that, because I always thought of myself as being a year or more behind everyone else when it came to understanding what they liked to call "real life," so, no, I was in no position, even in my fancy, to be a victimizer. I was a retard in "real life," even if I was intellectually smarter than all the people who seemed to take it in stride.

I guess I was just too *noble*. With Wendy I was just too good, or was that just too scared? I assumed that of all the guys in grade ten, I was the only one who was still a virgin. I figured, at least from what I had heard, that hardly any of the girls were. Maybe Doreen. No, there was Tony Gludovitz's story about Doreen Schmeck in the boys' changing room at the beach in Osoyoos. I did not believe this story, but I imagined it just the same.

And was Jeanette a virgin? Somehow, somewhere in the bottom of my filing cabinet in the back of my head, I had a hunch there was something wrong in Jeanette's past, something I would like to step into, find the bad person, and heroically avenge her. Even if it was a member of her family. There were no rumours that I knew of, so I was probably making a little legend out of my unorganized reading and the assumptions I was making about her clothing and food and shelter.

What did they call them in school — the necessities, the basics, the something or other, meaning everyone had to have them. Food, clothing, and shelter. I would have added baseball and books. When I got to my thirties I always listed jazz, baseball, beer, and Mexican food. But it looked to me as if Jeanette MacArthur was not doing all that well in any of those original basic categories. Her clothes looked as if they might have belonged to someone else some time ago, her house was missing some pieces, and I was pretty sure I had seen her stealing food. I had hardly ever seen her eating, and then only vegetables or fruit held in her hand.

I am pretty sure that I would have been told by a good number of adults to mind my own business, and I also think that the majority of them would have called themselves and each other Christians in those days. Among the things that I was sort of embarrassed by was that I could not get the idea of Jesus and all that out of my head. Well, when I was four I thought that there was a chance that I might be Jesus come back. Later I became infatuated with his radical notions — return evil with good, be generous to strangers, all that stuff. So it got so that I could not just ignore Jeanette. If I was going to be Detective Boy, I would be the Nazarene sleuth.

And a secret benefactor. For some reason I loved that idea. In the winter when we were in grade eight at school it snowed several times, and every time it snowed, Will and I would take our parents' brooms and sweep the snow off strangers' front steps and walks, then run before they noticed. Once we got caught and the housewife in the house forced us to take thirty cents. So we decided to give it to charity. But we could not find any charity, so we decided to get three ice cream cones, because Will's little brother Sandy was hanging around with us, and fill up our bodies with energy so that we could go back to the snow removal task with verve.

Later in life, when I found it important to be cryptic, I averred that the best revenge happened when the person who was the recipient of the revenge didn't notice. But when I was fourteen I figured that the best good deeds were the puzzling ones, when no one ever found out who had done them.

It wasn't all that hard to find out what a student's locker number was. Actually, when I got to Jeanette's locker, I was kind of surprised that she had a lock. We had to pay two dollars for them at the beginning of the school year, and I guess I thought that she would just have to have a closed door and hope that no one took any of her stuff. Even Jeanette had to have stuff.

I had made two dollars and forty cents at the bowling alley the night before, and was intent on my mission. The forty cents I would keep, partly because of the noise factor, and partly because the new issue of *Baseball Digest* had been at the corner store for two weeks. I waited until five minutes after my math class had started, till no one else was in the hallway, and then I folded my two-dollar bill twice and slipped it through the vent in Jeanette's locker.

Oh, no, I thought, what if this isn't her locker?

What if she doesn't notice the two-dollar bill falling onto the floor when she opens the door?

Then I had to decide whether to lurk after school and watch her at her locker, or just take off. Maybe she wouldn't even visit her locker before she went home. I didn't know what she had in there. Once I had walked by and noticed that she didn't have pictures from magazines taped to the inside walls and door, the way other girls did — pictures of movie stars, most of them women. I didn't see Veronica Lake on any girl's locker door, so

I knew that I had a lot more good taste and individualism than any of them.

Back when I was eleven or twelve I decided to start buying movie magazines, and I even went to The Hub pool hall and brought back a few issues of *Modern Screen* and *Photoplay*. I couldn't figure out the title of *Photoplay*. I figured that each issue should have the screenplay of a movie in it, but mainly it had pictures of Irene Dunne with an elaborate hairdo.

But pretty soon I gave up on movie magazines, and started buying sports magazines. For Christmas 1948 my parents bought me a subscription to *Sport*, which was twenty-five cents an issue in The Hub. I bought second-hand copies off Bill Redman, so I could keep my copies intact and still rip out full-page pictures for my bedroom wall in the basement. Gene Beardon and Joe Louis and Eddie Arcaro.

But I never put a *Sport* magazine picture in my locker. My locker had a picture of Wendy in it, so I didn't open it when anyone else was around. And there were a few paperback westerns on the shelf, maybe *Bullet Breed* by Leslie Ernenwein, published by Bantam Books.

Sometimes in westerns, when a character was expostulating, the author would say, "... he ejaculated."

I always liked to know what books people were reading. My father's favourite authors seemed to be Erle Stanley Gardner and Thorne Smith. I made a point of reading some Gardner things — they were always called the case of the something or other, but it was intimated to me that I didn't want to be reading Thorne Smith, and by golly, I didn't read him till I had grown up, and when I did I found out that I really liked that humour. I understood my dad's grin while he was turning the pages of *Turnabout*.

My mother liked to read books from the lending library, novels by authors I had never heard of, and she still does. My sister may have read some girls' books when she was a teenager, but she married a non-reader and got out of the habit herself. Wendy was reading mainly English comic novels published in paperback by Penguin Books, ugly things with small type and narrow gutters and no pictures on the cover. Drab good taste, I guess you would call it. I had no idea what Miss Verge liked to read, at least not till later. As for Jeanette MacArthur, well, that is where George Bowering, Boy Detective, needed to make his appearance.

RIGHT AFTER SCHOOL I was supposed to head home and fill the hoppers of the furnace and the kitchen stove with sawdust. The garage had no car in it, only a pile of sawdust from the sawmill. That was our fuel, and I was our fueler. Our kitchen stove would also take firewood, so I had to keep the woodbox full as well, and if there was a pile of split wood, which my father would do because he knew that I was not to be trusted with an axe, I had to add the sticks to the woodpile.

I kind of liked making a woodpile. You had to start one end with a sort of square tower of crossed sticks, and keep it at least as high as the tower at the other end and the piled sticks between them. It was neat work. I always had to find something neat about my jobs. When I was thinning apples in someone's orchard, I always pretended that the little beginner apples were the enemy, and I would fell their soldiers while rescuing their prisoners, which were the central little apple in the cluster you were cutting down to one. When you finished, hundreds of defeated little apples lay on the ground under the tree. Ones you could step on with your running shoes and feel on the bottom of your foot. Well, that was neat.

But it was a nice spring day, and I thought that I could take a chance that my parents wouldn't want the furnace on tonight. They were fond of saving money wherever they could, and it was not always sixty-eight degrees in our house in the spring or fall.

So instead of running down the hill to our place after school, I headed over to Fairview Road, which I figured Jeanette would descend on her way to Sawmill Road. Then I just hung around the bottom end of the bridge, trying to read a few pages, maybe from *Buckaroo's Code* by Wayne D. Overholser.

I thought that I was wasting my time. I *was* wasting my time, a lot of people would think. But eventually I saw her leave the gravelly school grounds, cross Fairview, and approach the wooden bridge. She noticed me on the one occasion that she raised her head from its scanning of the ground in front of her. Two years earlier I had heard her tell another girl that once in a while you will find a coin if you keep your eyes on the ground in front of you.

I was tempted to figure out where she was going to walk so I could drop a dime now and then.

When she got to the bottom end of the bridge I fell into step with her, but she kept her eyes down.

"You want something, Sport?" she asked, not looking at me.

"I want to ask you a question," I said, keeping my head up so I could warn her if any danger were to approach.

"I thought you already knew everything, Sport."

Why, I asked myself, was she browned off at me? I tended to think of myself as innocent, innocent with a touch of stupid. I tried to be sensitive, but then I was conflicted by the equal demands of sensitivity and forthrightness. I counted ten steps. Her steps were equal to mine in time and distance.

"What are you reading nowadays?" I asked her.

We were walking downhill on the sidewalk side of Fairview Road, so our steps went ka-plunk, ka-plunk.

"*Macbeth*," she said, face downward.

Five steps this time.

"No, I mean outside of school assignments. What are you reading, you know, just for yourself?"

I think she counted four steps.

"I don't read for myself, Sport. I read for other people. Like schoolteachers."

I guess I had come to realize that there were some boys who did not read books they didn't have to read. The guys on the basketball team, for instance. But I had somehow always supposed that since the girls usually got the best marks in school, they were readers.

"Where are you going?" asked Jeanette, and I could not read the tone in her voice, not exactly, but it didn't sound warm or interested.

"It's a free country," I said lightsomely. "I thought I'd walk along this way."

"You think it's a free country?"

"That's what they're always telling me."

"Well, have a happy dream," she said, this time lifting her face and looking straight at me.

I didn't know where this was going. But I was interested. I didn't know why. I wouldn't have been interested in a conversation with most of the people in my class at school — wouldn't be interested much in finding out about their family life or anything else about them. I hadn't been in all that many people's houses — Will's and Wendy's and a few others.

At a quick glance you could have thought that Jeanette would not be an exception to that rule. She had dull hair, dull skin, dull clothes, and no book in her hands. But I wanted to get inside the circle she had drawn in the air around her.

The brown and maroon skirt she was wearing came to the bottoms of her thin calves, and it was uneven at its hem. You could not see the shape of her bum. You could not see the shape of her chest that was presumably inside the brownish shirt she was wearing. She kept the buttons all done up. Her shoes were scuffed. Her ankles were of normal size, and she wore some kind of brown or dark green socks instead of white bobby socks. I could watch her for an hour and never get a bit of a hard on, pardon my French, and I had never once felt like kissing her thin lips.

I kicked stones as we walked along the street leading to Sawmill Road. The streets in Oliver had names and numbers, but they weren't posted — they were only recorded on charts inside some back room at the village hall. Maybe people's houses had numbers assigned to them, but you never saw a number on a house. You might see a sign with a name burnt into it. The Borks, for example, thought that the plural of their name, as it should appear on the sign beside their front door, was "The Bork's."

"My dreams are pretty much like my life," I said. "Relatively happy. I am determined to have a happy childhood."

"So you are still a child?"

"I hope so. I'm not in any hurry to become 'mature'. I have heard enough of 'mature' to last me a lifetime." I did not tell her that it was a word I often heard from my mother and sometimes heard from Wendy.

She didn't get it. At least she didn't laugh.

"Sometimes we have to grow up before we want to," she said, without looking at me. Here, I thought, we are onto something.

But I did not know how to get from sentence to sentence in this kind of conversation. I still don't, if you want to know. I kept believing, and maybe still do, that we can think back and forth. Sometimes I have had that experience — call it telepathy if you like — and I have always liked it, even when what we were thinking about was not all that pleasant.

Now she started walking faster. I walked faster to keep up. Then she broke into a run. I didn't run after her. I didn't want anyone to see such a thing.

I saw Ritchie Schneider in the yard of the packing house. I waved at him, but he didn't wave back. He had bowled a game under two hundred last week.

⌇

I TOOK MY time walking back up to town. It was four blocks, to our place, all uphill, and when I got there I was supposed to mow the lawn. I had been told to mow the lawn three days before.

"I'm expecting rain," I had said then.

"It hasn't rained in four months," my mother reminded me.

"I'll get right at it," I said. "Oh," I said, "I have to mail a letter right today or it'll be too late for the contest." I was hoping to win a cash prize for naming the new hockey team in Kamloops. "I'll get right at it when I get back from the post office."

"I am looking forward to it," said my mother, demonstrating her enthusiasm by the way she chopped the cabbage for tonight's coleslaw.

"Unless it's raining," I said.

The warm spring sunshine was prying cherry blossoms open in orchards north and south of town, and as I walked up the hill toward home I undid my top two shirt buttons. I think guys were doing this all over the valley. As summer approached buttons were undone, and by the time summer was here, most of the boys and men would have their shirts off more often than they had them on. We were a tanned populace.

When I got to the main street I stopped at the corner in front of Tuck's Cafe and looked up the sidewalk and across at the front of the Orchard Cafe, behind which the town's other pool hall did a brisk business. That was where we white kids watched Manuel Louie and Windy Bone show off their trick shots and cool moves. We imitated them, rehearsing the gestures we admired so much. Windy Bone's favourite show was to make his cue ball stick and then to shoot at balls that were still moving. I saw him clean a table off the break like that more than once.

I split my pool hall time between the Orchard and Frank's, over on this side of the street. At fifteen I was an illegal in the pool hall, and being the boy I was I was both exhilarated and morally uneasy about the fact. I was not a particularly good shot, either.

Next to Tuck's Cafe was the door that opened to the staircase up to Miss Verge's apartment. In the crosswalk was Miss Verge, carrying a briefcase filled with books and papers, one would think, and she was on her way home after school. I watched as she walked, briskly, solid, like tuna in a can. Halfway across the street, which was a domesticated section of Highway 97, her eyes found mine, and she looked right at me the rest of the way across. She did not smile, but she gave me a friendly look that a smile might have rested on. Her eyes picked up the fact that my top two shirt buttons were undone. I didn't care — this was out of school.

"Come with me," she said, still walking.

"Huh?" was my measured response.

"I need you to do something for me."

The street door was unlocked when we went in, but once we were inside Miss Verge locked it.

"You know the way," she said, and this time she followed me up the stairs. I remembered looking at her legs and behind, and imagined her looking at mine. But why? Who ever heard of a teacher looking at a boy's legs and so on?

She handed me her briefcase while she unlocked her apartment door, then stood back to let me go in. That felt funny because as a boy of that time I knew enough to stand back and let a woman, or an adult, or the person whose place this is, go in first. But in I went. I looked around for a place to put the briefcase, but I also liked the idea of holding it. Nothing bad would happen if I was holding a briefcase against my chest. Inside my chest I could feel my heart beating. It must have been the staircase.

Imagine that. Here I was, a lad much brighter than his classmates — not as proficient at class grades but better read and more perceptive — and I was flummoxed to be in a single woman schoolteacher's flat. I should have had some witty repartee at the ready, my stock in trade. But I was a wordless goof with a briefcase and a beating heart.

I have no idea whether Miss Verge knew any of this. She quietly took the briefcase from me and put it on the floor beside a small desk she had snugged against a back wall. Then she took my elbow and led me toward the Venetian blind window overlooking the street where I would often walk by, talking too loudly and otherwise clowning around.

Miss Verge pointed upward, and when she did so her pointing finger was barely as high as the top of my head. Her white blouse pulled slightly loose of the waistband on her navy blue pleated skirt.

What she wanted me to do for her had something to do with the fact that she was a pretty short human being and I was tall, though somewhat gawky. It seems that she wanted to give her Venetian blinds their annual cleaning, and there was no way she was going to be able to do that unless they were taken down and lugged into the bathroom, where she would fill the tub with sudsy hot water.

"You'll have to stand on the windowsill and reach up," she said. "I'll be here to support you, and you can hand me down the blinds."

"But the street, I'll look stupid —"

"Don't worry. It's late afternoon. The sun will be shining right on the window. All anyone will be able to see outside is a reflection."

"Are you sure?"

"I'm a teacher."

"Well —"

"Okay, hop up there. Don't hang on to the blinds. Grab the wood along the side, and I will support you."

This is a conversation I have never mentioned to anyone until now.

"Okay, up you go. I've got you. There you are."

I was standing in my draped corduroys, my half-open shirt and my ankle-high running shoes, on a windowsill overlooking Highway 97 on a sunny afternoon, and just beneath the floor were my friends shooting eight ball and drinking NuGrape soda pop. And Miss Verge was holding the backs of my thighs. Don't get me wrong — without her help I probably would have fallen from the windowsill. At first I was not certain of her ability to keep me up there, but I was really not surprised by her strength. I had seen her on the badminton court, after all. I knew the muscularity of her legs and arms. I soon forgot my worry and turned my attention to disconnecting the Venetian blind apparatus from its moorings.

But then her hands ascended the backs of my thighs a little. Probably to get a grip with better leverage. But then her left hand was on the back of my thigh, and her right hand was really more on my bum than on my thigh.

"Are you all right there?" she asked, and I had to assume that whatever she was doing was just in the interest of my safety.

"Sure," I said. "It's just that I haven't seen how these things are connected before. I'll get it."

"Take your time," she suggested. "You don't want to hurry things and mess it up."

I felt her move, as if she were taking a little step. And then her right hand had come around between my legs and was holding me in front!

You know what was happening to me physically. Her small hand was full. I felt how strong she was. She did not move her hand now, only held on. I was behind a mirror, I told myself, and then I could not perform any more thought. Nor did I say anything. Who could have thought of anything to say? My adolescent mind was emptied of facts, that this was a schoolteacher from my high school, that I was fifteen and she was "mature," that the sky was blue for a reason and that there were fish at the deepest part of the ocean. I would have ejaculated warmly into her hand if it had not been for corduroy and the cotton under the corduroy.

I was able, at last, to bring down the blind and lay it on the carpetted floor. I did not know where to direct my eyes.

"Would you like some apple juice, or maybe some cocoa?" asked Miss Verge. "You don't drink coffee yet, do you?"

"No, thank you," I managed to murmur.

"Would you like to use the bathroom before you go home?" asked Miss Verge.

"Yes, please," I said.

⌒

THANK GOODNESS IT was not teachers' bowling night that night. And I was the recipient of another stroke of luck. My mother was doing the laundry in her ringer washing machine, so I ducked into my room, changed underwear and pants, and chucked my cords and briefs into the swirling soapy water.

"I believe," said my mother, "I have told you this before. Whites and coloureds don't go in together."

"Just like in Alabama?" I asked.

"What are you talking about? Those underpants are white and those slacks are green."

"They are? Green? I thought they were blue." I was gradually learning about my colourblindness.

"The woodbox could use filling," she said.

After supper (meatloaf — yum!) I pretty well stayed in my room. I played a week's worth of my homemade big league baseball game, and finally the St. Louis Browns fell out of first place. I wrote a letter to my pen pal in England, Roger Bunting, telling him all about the St. Louis Browns, this in answer to a letter from him telling me all about Tottenham Hotspur. Then I settled down and read right through to the end of *Texas Triggers* by Eugene Cunningham.

At one point, I pulled my pyjamas open and checked my little one out. He was just lying there, a little comma. I smiled at him and went back to reading. Strangely, I didn't think of Miss Verge's apartment at all.

I SAID MY prayers every night before I went to sleep in those days. I didn't kneel by the bed the way you would see kids do in magazine advertisements or family movies. I would just lie in bed and address myself to God. When we were really little, my mother, I guess it must have been, taught my sister and me to say, "Now I lay me down to sleep. I pray, the Lord, my soul to keep." I never could figure that one out. I thought that it meant that I was asking God to keep my soul. This might have been the earliest conflict I noticed between grammar and religion. "If I should die before I wake, I pray, the Lord, my soul to take." Maybe it was a three-way tussle — religion, grammar, and poetry, because "God bless Mom and Dad and Sally and Grandpa and Grandma" violated the metric. As I grew a little older I would add people upon whom blessings should be bestowed. I didn't really know what was entailed in the verb "bless," but I figured that it was something like allowing them to go on living with a kind of godly umbrella over them.

By the age of fifteen I had quit going to Sunday school, not noticing that I was quitting, and I didn't go to the United Church, which was upstairs from Sunday school. Sometimes I went with Wendy to the Anglican church. A couple of things there bothered me, though I didn't know why — at some point everyone in the pews said something about believing in the Catholic Church, and you had to kneel down when you were praying. At least they didn't swing incense in Wendy's church. She told me that in the high Anglican Church they swing incense and carry out other rituals that I considered kind of like idol worshipping. I wasn't too crazy about popes and all that either, not because of my less formalized religion, but because of my sincere belief in democracy. Well, I guess that was connected to my religion, too. The more puritan you get the more democratic you get. As long as you don't force your convictions on anyone else.

(Whoa! This is getting to be a lecture rather than the story of my adolescence, though I guess an autobiography has room for telling readers about one's beliefs and misapprehensions.)

So what I'm saying is that when I was a child and when I was an adolescent, I believed in sin. I wasn't analytical enough to separate sin from wrongdoing. But I did want to be exact. I mean I was not going to smoke. I was not going to drink liquor. I was not going to steal or curse or lie. I thought that the Ten Commandments and the Golden Rule were logical and decent, and that the life lived according to them made good sense.

Once when I was five I asked my mother whether there was ever a time when you could tell a lie.

"If you need to in order to keep someone out of great danger," she said.

That was my first lesson in relativism. But I knew that there were unbending flinthearts in the world. In grade one we used to retell jokes containing preachers who yelled angrily about bad behaviour on the part of little kids. They would holler in the pulpit about children who took each other's clothes off, or took the

Lord's name in vain.

That was another thing I wondered about. If you tried in vain to teach a cat to fetch your slippers, that meant that you were unsuccessful. So taking the Lord's name in vain — first of all, what did "taking" mean, and secondly, where was the failure?

Anyway, somehow or another the kids in a small town will eventually hear about the strictest rules laid down by someone else's preachers. The Jehovah's Witness kids weren't supposed to read any books except the Bible. The Lutheran kids were not supposed to listen to the hit parade. The Holy Roller girls could not use lipstick. The Catholic kids could commit sins all they wanted to, because all they had to do was confess them to the priest and start all over again, clean as a whistle.

Some preachers said it was a mortal sin to play with your wiener. Or look up a girl's skirt. Or accidentally feel your sister's tits. We heard about sinful magazines that showed pictures of bare-naked women standing or lying in sexy poses, but no one ever seemed to be able to find one. I had somehow come into possession of a copy of *Sunbathing for Health* magazine. It was full of gray and white pictures of nude people doing archery or volleyball outdoors. The tits were there to see, but the hairy parts were airbrushed out. I felt a little bit nervous about having this magazine hidden in the basement, but I don't think I felt sinful, actually. I still have it. It's in a box with my 1950 issues of *Sport* magazine.

Some guys carried typed and folded dirty stories in their wallets, and once in a while we would carefully unfold them and read about guys scoring. One title I remember well was "Behind the Green Door." I think that the guys who wrote and sang the song with that name in 1956 knew about this bit of *samizdat*. There were also little square black and white sex comics in which Wimpy would screw a scrawny woman in exchange for hamburgers, or Blondie would let the dogs screw her. I spent a lot of my time drawing cartoon faces, and I also got pretty good at drawing tits. It wasn't that I had seen any. I copied Al Capp's drawings of Daisy Mae, and especially Moonbeam McSwine. The latter, you'll remember, used to recline in the pigpen, wearing torn shorts and a blouse tied in front, her arm around a hog. Sometimes I thought about her while I was choking my chicken.

I did, don't get me wrong, get wind of the notion that sin and sex were connected with each other. Of course for the longest time I thought the word "sex" was a designation as to whether you were a boy or a girl, but I did catch on. Then it became a charged and exciting word, though a little repulsive. It was like the word "breasts." You know what I mean. A lot of boys could never say the word "vagina" once they had heard or read it.

When I was about eleven I read the word "rape" in a novel by Zane Grey, and I knew that it was something awful but something I wasn't supposed to know. In another Zane Grey novel a bad guy tears the shirt off a woman and she blushes from the belt up. Jeepers, I thought, am I supposed to be reading this?

So it used to be that I had two different lives going, the one in the village of Oliver, BC, and the one in books and magazines. But now it was beginning to appear that I had to lead three different lives in Oliver, each of them a secret from the other two. To this day I don't understand how I could be such a yearning virgin with Wendy, for example, after having an adult woman make me spurt inside my trousers. Or how I could be a heroic protector of riverside Jeanette if I was also the innocent erotic charge of a perspiration-shining racquet woman?

I still have not reasoned these disparities out. Maybe that is why I have to write this little backcountry autobiography.

Anyway, I did believe in sin, or maybe we should call it doing wrong. I believed in wrong and right, but I did not connect

Wendy's small breasts with sin or wrong. I was not given to long periods of analysis during which I tried to ascertain the presence and relative percentages of my mixed attitudes. It was just that when I undid Wendy's shirt and saw the gentle rise of her skin, I felt as if I were being afforded a look at beauty while experiencing a taboo that she was equally ambivalent about.

You see the kind of language you get into when you try to say something honest about your feelings? Women are always, so the cliché goes, trying to get you to talk about your feelings. But don't talking and feelings take place in two widely separated worlds? Like dreams — everyone knows that you can not find words to properly narrate your dreams. You have to find equivalents, maybe.

Clouds. Puppies. Sunsets. Swans. Baseballs. Snowscapes. Roses. 1996 Nackenheimer Rothenberg Riesling Spätlese Gunderloch.

But no. At this very moment I am remembering the moment after I removed Wendy's small brassiere. If you could only see!

My god, she was cool skin from the waist of her homemade blue or green skirt up. How I waited till I leaned to touch. Her chin was up. Her eyes were closed. Her head was tilted back. I touched her tiny nipple with my lips. I touched it with the end of my tongue. I was kind of scared.

I returned to kissing her lips, licking her crooked tooth.

I just let her put her bra and shirt back on, and we walked up the dirt road through the orchard toward her grey house. We planned our wedding and the name of our first baby. It would be Dorothy. Or Theodore. Dorothy was my dead aunt's name. Theodore was the name I wished I had been given.

When I got home I went downstairs and looked at my favourite pages in *Sunbathing for Health*.

I CAN'T HONESTLY tell you whether the notion of sin ever occurred to me when it came to Jeanette MacArthur. I thought it was the noble, romantic, heroic part of me that had me waiting for her at the Fairview Road bridge. That's kind of a flip adult way of characterizing my silly adolescent state, but then again, when I was four I thought that I might be the second coming of Christ.

I hope that you will agree that we more sensitive teenagers grew up surrounded by irony. After some US popular psychologist claimed that comic books were turning kids into criminals, parents all over the place tried to keep them out of our hands. Nowadays, when teenagers carry cocaine in one pocket and a cell phone you can download fellatio movies from in the other, comic books don't seem so scary. In fact comic books are no longer to be found in drugstores. You have to go to a comic book store and hang around with all the twenty-eight-year-old men under unpopular haircuts.

What I mean by irony is this: I learned my desire for a moral world from two printed sources — the New Testament and *Detective Comics*. In the latter, Bruce Wayne had a mansion in which he kept a teenaged boy whose working clothes included short shorts. Jesus mainly hung out with a group of men, except for the woman who might have been called, years down the line, a fag hag. None of that bothered me. I kind of liked being a secret good guy. I can't remember how I squared that with the secret night-time window of the packing house, through which I could squirm on my way to one free bottle of green pop from their faulty machine. The packing house, by the way, was down at the beginning of Sawmill Road, along which Jeanette MacArthur and maybe her mysterious father lived.

Or was it her father? This is where George Bowering, Master Sleuth came in. I could ask Jeanette clever questions that would have her giving me information without noticing, or I could be a quiet sleuth in the shadows. Well, I had done that, and all I'd seen was an underprivileged girl cooking a potato.

What would be the crime in asking her some questions? Is friendly inquisitiveness a sin?

"Hey, Jeanette, have you thought of what you're going to do after you're finished with high school?"

"That is exactly none of your beeswax, Sport."

So, okay, maybe it was a sin. A less noble person than myself would have said to hell with it and headed for the pool hall. Sometimes I looked out into the surrounding world and envied all those people who did not feel themselves chosen to improve the world. Why did I have to be a rescuer and a crusader? Why did I have to spend Halloween night going around fixing things that other boys disassembled or soaped over? Well, at least I *thought* about doing that on Halloween night, and at least I didn't do any of those destructive things myself. Well, except for the time in grade four when I helped three other guys shove over the outhouse in Mr. Eisenhut's orchard. I was a new kid in the valley — later, for sure, I would more than make up for tipping over this outhouse by pulling weeds in old ladies' gardens.

Except on days when I had to be at the bowling alley by four o'clock, I usually waited for Jeanette at the Fairview Road bridge. If she'd wanted to take a longer way around she could have avoided me, but as it was, she would just keep her head down and keep walking, not acknowledging me when I fell into step beside her. She could have pushed me into the path of a car gunning it up Fairview. But she didn't.

Eventually, in the first days of June, she got to lifting her head as we walked, and then one day we stopped and sat on an old wooden loading platform in front of a scrabbly orchard just south of the juice plant. Long grass showed above the uneven surface of the boards. A broken wooden picking ladder, probably a twelve-footer, lay on its side in the grass. Jeanette was wearing a greyish-brown skirt, and as she sat beside me with her feet dangling I could see the bare skin of her knees. They were halfway through their transformation from little girl knees to young woman knees. That was another thing I generally liked better than the knees you see on the women's underwear pages of the Eaton's catalogue.

For the first time that I could remember, she spoke first.

"Are you really as stupid as you make yourself out to be, Bowering?"

"I'll stack my stupidity up against anyone's," I retorted, pretty satisfied with my insular wit.

"It gets pretty boring, you know."

"Okay," I allowed, "I could tell you why I joke around the way I do, but this isn't about me. It's about you."

"What is it? What's about me?"

Her guard was suddenly down, and there was a little alarm in her voice. I decided to take a chance and look right at her. I just caught a little fright leaving her plain face. Actually, it was plain with a touch of what we used to call cute, something you could pick up when she turned her head, a flash of eye and lips at once, before it was gone again and you were left with a few freckles over a nose that was a little too bony.

If I were acting my normal way at this juncture, I would have rolled my eyes and lifted my hands and adopted an "Inner Sanctum" voice to make broad hints about a conspiracy centring on her and her mean home. But maybe I didn't want to compromise my ongoing investigation. I cooled it.

"Oh," I said after a long second, "this conversation."

"Are we having a conversation, Chum?"

"Yeah, I guess. If you don't mind."

"What would you like to talk about?"

And that made it difficult. I was bashful. Of course I wanted to get the conversation around to her secret life. No, that was too dramatic. What? I was worried about dramatic? What was going on here? This was just Jeanette MacArthur, a loner girl who never had the money for a Creamsicle.

"I am open to suggestions," I said at last.

She was no longer lowering her head or looking the other way. Her gaze became so strong that I had to turn my head. I kicked my feet that were hanging over the side of the platform.

"How about why you are following me?"

"Not following. Waiting. Walking with you."

"How come you are sticking money in my locker? That was you, wasn't it? Why do you do that?"

"Once. I did it once."

"I found a dollar in my socials text. What do you think you're buying with a dollar, Pal?"

I was something like humiliated. I was very uncomfortable. I did not say anything. I could not think of a word that would not make things worse. Jeanette got up, and didn't brush the dust off her skirt. She jumped off the platform, and I scrambled to follow.

"I thought if you were —"

"What? What?"

"I thought if you were a little short for, you know, lunch money, I could help a bit this once."

She walked fast and I walked fast, trying to catch up. She turned and stared at me.

"You know what you can do, Bowering?"

"No —"

"You can piss off."

This time I just stood there as she walked beside the narrow old pavement of Sawmill Road. I was a speechless boy. It was the first time I had ever heard a girl say piss.

"GOD BLESS MOM and Dad and Sally and Roger and Jimmy and Grandpa and Wendy and Jeanette," I asked that night.

Once I found a ten-dollar bill folded twice as if it had been in a woman's purse, though it did not smell as nice as any money that had ever been in my mother's purse would. It was on the sidewalk in front of the Food Basket grocery store. Sometimes, when I remembered that moment, I would walk with my head down, just in case there was money on the ground. In the whole area in and around Oliver there had to be some money on the ground all the time. I began to fantasize that Jeanette would find a twenty-dollar bill or maybe something bigger, though I figured that anything bigger was unlikely to be on the ground. Not around this town, anyway. I kind of even prayed that she would find a twenty, maybe two twenties folded together.

I almost felt as if I were doing something good.

CHAPTER 9

THE 24TH OF May used to be a big demonstrative holiday in Oliver. If you were still a kid in elementary school, you would probably have to be in the maypole dance. A white shirt and a pair of dark shorts, oh please, and all that skippitty skip and that aura of British royalty. I mean even then I was not fond of the monarchy, though when you see me at three years old I'm wearing a sweatshirt with a picture of a bulldog standing on a Union Jack and the words "Britons never will be slaves."

Now the gramophone player is wound up tight and there is a long vooom growing louder and louder and then that sappy skippity song, "oh lassies and lads let go of your dads," or whatever, and away we went, impersonating Britons on the round rocks of the Oliver elementary school playground. Each kid held the end of a ribbon, one colour or the other, and tried not to goof up the pattern as they intertwined while skipping around the pole, braiding their ribbons and bringing tears to their parents' eyes.

It would be interesting to poll all your grade three classmates and ask them when they realized that they had been urchins performing an annual sexual ritual in celebration of spring's concupiscence during these festivities. I was so embarrassed at the time, (and I think that at least all the boys were), but I wish now that I could go back and lurk under a tree and watch us dancing around that colourful maypole.

By the time that grade ten was over we had been long freed from that colonial nonsense and those short pants, and now the school's 24th of May was integrated into the town's celebrations, so we had a track meet and a parade with flowers all over the fire truck and all the related smalltown effort. The first fruit would not be coming off the trees for another two or three weeks, so unlike the Labour Day weekend, there would be no natural celebration of agriculture and its gods. The 24th of May was a long dead English queen's fictional birthday, but here in the semi-arid South Okanagan Valley, it was the day when the public swimming pool opened and school was closed down for a day of sweat and flowers.

I always tried to get out of the track meet after I won the red ribbon in grade seven for coming in third in the sixty-yard dash. John Lundy won the white ribbon for second place, and I can't remember who got the blue ribbon. There were only three of us in this race. It was the only time I had ever won a ribbon.

Now in grade ten I had the perfect excuse. I was supposed to be covering the athletic events for the Oliver *Chronicle*. Wearing my green fedora perched on the back of my head, I carried a coiled secretary's notebook and one of those newfangled ballpoint pens as I stood beside the sawdust pit where highjumpers landed with a little yelp.

"Nice try," I said.

"Up yours, Bowering," came the replies.

A loudspeaker mounted on the roof of a pickup truck made incomprehensible sounds originating from a human throat.

While the early heats for the two hundred were being run I ambled over to the area occupied by several plywood booths. At one of them you could rent some medium-sized wooden rings and try to cast them in such a way that they came to rest around the neck of an empty milk bottle and earned you a cheap stuffed doll for your sweetheart or mom. In this way the Benevolent and Protective Order of Elks collected donations to their Save the Children Fund. At other booths you could try to throw darts at balloons, or softballs at stacked imitation milk bottles. Among all these charitable stalls was the kissing booth. There for fifty cents you could get a more or less peremptory kiss from a young woman who was in actuality a married woman that everyone knew. The kissing booth gave rise to a lot of jocularity, guys using their boots to kick their other boots. If this had been a comic strip, someone would have been saying "Pshaw!"

I had fifty cents, but I couldn't see spending it on a kiss from Shirley Woods's big sister. I felt good about the charity — the kiss money was going to the March of Dimes, five dimes at a smack. But these people ten years older than I were guffawing and giggling, and I wondered — really, was this what kissing and adulthood are all about in this valley so far from the real thing? By "the real thing" I meant things such as you'd find in magazines and books from some big city in the eastern USA.

I walked around the kissing booth looking for a place where I could sit and jot down something about the activity in this section of the grounds, and bumped into Miss Verge.

"Sorry, excuse me," I said. I had the notebook in my left hand and the ballpoint pen in the other.

"Are you all right?" she replied, and I noticed that she was taking her arm away from my waist.

"Sure," I said, protecting myself with my patented smart-aleck voice. "I've just escaped from the kissing booth."

"I saw you there. You had the oddest look on your face."

"It was a key moment in my juvenile years," I said, standing there with a notebook and a ballpoint pen.

My eyes shifted. We were behind the booths, the only two people in the area. Behind me I could hear faint sounds of banging and popping and female laughter.

"I can imagine," she said, and stepped closer — so close that we were almost touching, like people talking in a television drama, not that I had at that time ever seen a television drama. Here I am, babbling in print, a lexical equivalent of the way I was feeling at the time — trapped, intrigued, in a panic, desirous, dizzy.

"Uh," I managed to say, stuck for the next syllable, a writer boy with a ballpoint pen and no words.

"I think that you deserve one for free," she said, and she stood on her toes.

"I, uh —"

She put her left hand on the back of my head and pulled it down, stood on her toes and kissed my mouth. I was too horrified to try escaping. No, not horrified. Something else. Too something to try escaping.

I had kissed girls. Wendy's tongue had flicked against mine for a half-second. I was not really a good kisser. I knew that. I had been told that, if you have to know. Miss Verge's warm mouth was open and moving. Her tongue forced my mouth open and then entered me the way a devil might enter a soul. I had to move my tongue too, and just hoped that I did it right. She nearly swallowed my mouth, and now I noticed that because she was standing on her toes, her muscular thighs were against mine. I had my eyes wide open, looking out for witnesses. I did not drop my notebook and ballpoint pen, not even when her hand pressed against me. My cock was down one pant leg, and her hand was against it, her palm and short fingers holding it now, and then she stepped away. I nearly fell on my face in the long grass.

I think I was holding onto my notebook and ballpoint pen not as symbols of my chosen profession, but because I didn't know what I would do with my hands if they were empty.

This was frightening, of course. What if a kid or a parent or a teacher were to come behind the booths and see us? Sure, Miss Verge would be in trouble, but I didn't want to be involved in it, and there was a particular problem with that trouble — my father was a teacher at the school. It would be a problem for him that I could not manage to envision, and it would be a problem for me as the son of the teacher.

But fright was not my only sensation. When you are a boy of fifteen, or so it seemed back in those innocent days, just about everything is a sex object — all schoolgirls, various foods and food containers, mountaintop profiles, animals, holes in the ground, some items of clothing, vacuum cleaners, furniture. If a grade eleven girl had touched my cock I might not have been quite as scared as I was to have a teacher touch it, but I wonder whether I would have been as excited?

I figured that Miss Verge must have been crazy. Why else would she have kissed a schoolboy reporter at the fairgrounds? More important, what should I do in the face of this craziness? To tell the truth, I started to imagine what it would feel like if she took hold of my *bare* cock. In fact, that night and some nights after that I imagined such a possibility while I did what I did.

❧

AFTER THE 24TH of May we were really into summer in the South Okanagan. My cleaning job at the swimming pool was on again, and school seemed a little unreal. The windows were wide open to let in air and sound, but for those kids who had to write final exams, it was getting to be time to open those books again and really read them this time. My personal program was to achieve just high enough marks to be recommended rather than having to write the exams. There was a problem in English. I could not help myself when it came to the composition and grammar part. I always got a hundred in grammar exercises. So I had to pull my marks down a little when it came to the literature part. I could just about memorize several scenes from *The Renegade* by L.L. Foreman, but when it came to some poems by William Wordsworth, I would wander cloudy as a loner.

My mother was not pleased by this. Sometimes she would try to explain to me that I should put away my sports magazines and western novels and newspaper comics and concentrate on my school reading. I didn't really know how my father felt about it. When I think back I realize that he knew about some boys who did not voluntarily read anything, so I now assume, as I did back then, that he was not all that worried.

My extra-curricular reading went along with my loneness, as it still does. It contributed to it, I think. Sometimes it pissed people off. "Why the hell don't you *live* life instead of reading about it?" I think they might have been smart enough to think that my reading was somehow a criticism of their lives devoid of reading. But I just liked it. It gave me two lives running at the same time. Why would anyone turn that down?

Sometimes, of course, I caught hell for *what* I read. When I turned in a class report on Ray Bradbury's *The Martian Chronicles* I was chastized for wasting my time reading mere science fiction instead of say, Somerset Maugham. Mrs. Hodgins said that I was wasting a god-given brain, that once again I was not living up to my potential.

So I learned not to talk about what I was reading, except with my buddy Will, and occasionally with John Jalovec, who had read even more westerns than I had. I kept score for the basketball games and wrote them up for the *Herald*, but I knew better than to try to discuss books with the basketball players. I didn't even bother to wonder whether they read my stories of their exploits in the newspapers.

There were magazines and paperback books in the front part of The Hub, or as we called it, Frank's Pool Hall, but though I spent nearly as much time there as I did in the back room with all the tables, I never saw Frankie Fritz or Ritchie Schneider there. I bought my first book of poetry there, a drugstore paperback called *Poems for Men* by Damon Runyan. The poems were all about boxing and baseball and horse racing. I knew Damon Runyan from reading sports magazines, and now I was being slid without knowing it from teenage sports fandom into literature, kind of. In those magazines I first read Ring Lardner and John Lardner. They were showing me what I wanted to be when and if I grew up. I would be a sports writer for, say, the St. Louis *Post-Dispatch*. That was another neat thing about reading *Baseball Digest* — I got to know the names of all the big newspapers in that country I was going to move to as soon as I got old enough. Maybe I could get a job at the Cincinnati *Enquirer* or the Philadelphia *Inquirer*.

I was, I would bet, the only person in my school, including all the teachers, who knew about the Philadelphia *Inquirer*. And probably only John Jalovec and I knew what a *remuda* is.

Wendy was one of those people who didn't know all the things I knew.

"I'd sure like to have you in my *remuda*," I said.

"Well," she said, alarmingly resembling my mother, "I have you in my dishes clean-up. I will wash and you will dry."

This was soon after Sunday dinner at the Love house, as I

liked to call it. That is, it was now four p.m., and though Wendy's dad had gone back to the orchard to take care of something, we would have the rest of the afternoon to laze around — after the dishes were put away. Then we would all drive into town for Evensong.

Wendy insisted on doing dishes the Home Economics way, from right to left. At home we always did them left to right, like reading. I felt awkward, but I also felt sort of domestic, doing dishes with the girl I wanted to marry some day in the distant future. I kissed her ear while drying a saucer. Her lips parted a little and the air made a sound while going into her mouth. I decided to sing.

> *Mona Lisa, Mona Lisa*
> *Men have named you*
> *You're so like the lady*
> *With the mystic smile*

"There is a lot of style and feeling in the way you sing," said my fiancée, "but you do not hit the exact middle of the note, I must say."

She handed me a saucepan.

"What you were hearing right then was a blues chord," I said.

"You cannot sing a chord," she said, in a voice pretty well devoid of cruelty. She was the only person I knew who said "cannot." In fact she often spoke an English I had otherwise not encountered outside of books.

"What do you know about the blues?" I enquired, or perhaps inquired.

"I know that you give me the blues at least once a day."

"Does this have to do with becoming mature or not becoming mature?"

"That would be, I am coming to believe, an unlikely development."

"All I can tell you," I said, "is that the prospect of growing up and being an adult is not all that attractive to me."

"Are we here talking again about George Bowering the noble and romantic young lad?"

"I love you, Limey."

"I love you too, colonial savage."

OUTSIDE IN THE yard you had to look where you were going because the chickens were allowed to walk anywhere, and they just dropped their little dark grey bits with the white ends. That's the way sweethearts took a walk back in those days in those parts — heading out of the yard. The farther you got from the unpainted back steps and into the long-grass of the orchard, the less chicken shit there was, and the greater chance there was that I would be able to get inside Wendy's shirt. But her father was somewhere among the rows of trees, moving sprinkler pipes or cutting weeds. We tried to stay away from the rows where the sprinklers had been, because there would be hundreds of little slugs just about the shape of chicken shit all over the grass. And if there was any chance that I could get my teen angel to lie down it had to be somewhere dry, but not dusty.

And it had to be somewhere unseen by her father, the light-weight boxing champion of the Royal Navy. I had no idea whether he liked me at all. I knew that Wendy's mother liked me all right, because when I was around her I always acted as much like a grateful colonial boy as possible, either that or a right proper Limey lad, such as I had read about in *Boy's Own Annual*.

Truth be told, I was not as confident as I hoped to appear. For all my superiority I felt inferior. I knew all the English kids in town, but I was not a good friend of any of them. I had friends who came to the valley with their parents from Belgium and Yugoslavia and Austria, but none of them had fathers that wore blue blazers.

And I was not sure who Wendy was. She was a proper English girl with a teen costume that was not quite as good as her class-mates', and she spoke with a refined, we gathered, accent, and played the piano, and volunteered whenever young volunteers were invited. But when I put my hand on her warm little breast and she opened her mouth a little, I knew that there was some-thing really warm down in her — do you know what I mean? As if she could get out of control, and if this very controlled person ever got a little out of control, it would scare me or challenge me more than I might be able to stand.

There were those rumours, which I did not believe. Could not believe, not if I was to go on being the noble romantic boy or coward I knew myself to be. When I put my hand inside her little bra, she no longer pushed my fingers away, the way that girls were supposed to do for a while, but I always stopped there because it was the good thing to do, not to take advantage of her inability to protect herself from her own desire, because that was somewhere around down there.

We walked hand in hand between the trees, looking cute in case there were any adults that could see us. Aren't they a sweet pair, that Capulet and that other whatever? We walked down the slope of the orchard toward a spot we had come to think of as our own. The creek that formed a border with the next orchard meandered to a corner where the tree rows had to narrow toward a point, and a pair of lovers could lie in the grass and look up to see the branches of four Red Delicious apple trees converge. By September an ordinary eye could not tell which tree a certain piece of fruit belonged to.

And then we were on the warm grass and kissing one another. I lost all embarrassment about my kitchen haircut, and dared to try to kiss her the way Miss Verge had kissed me. Wendy pulled her head away and looked at me with suspicion, or at least interest, and returned her face to my pleasure. I set about kissing some more, and I heard her breath turn into a kind of moan, and I thought oh dear what have I done or rather what am I doing and do I really think that I can carry this off, and if I was such a bad kisser up till now I would for sure be bad at anything else, and what is a lad supposed to do about learning, where is Miss Verge when I need her, and soft, what lovely skin do my fingers now behold?

"Oh," breathed Miss Love, "we have to —"

"We are in your father's orchard on a Sunday afternoon, and it's not one of the biggest orchards in the Valley," I said, disengaging a little, my hard boyhood wondering why nobody was touching him or it.

"Ah, you are such a sensible bastard," she said.

"Such is my ambition betimes," I replied, trying to adjust my corduroy trousers without being noticed.

"You are a tease."

"Let us then be chaste," I offered. "You may correct my misassumptions regarding the history of the British monarchy or the pronunciation of the King's English."

"I love you, George. You may be sure of that, though I sometimes ask myself what I am doing with you."

"Ofttimes."

"Yes."

"I love you helplessly, hopelessly, but really, does that sound right, hopelessly? I hope to be with you for the remainder of my short life."

Short life was part of my idea about being noble and romantic.

"I want to be your life's companion, as they say," she said, her voice nearly drifting away. "But I want to know that you can be serious."

"You want me to be a doctor or a lawyer? I'm sorry. I cannot, as you would say, offer you that. Can you live seriously with a newspaper reporter?"

She was going to reply, but —

"Like Clark Kent," I added.

She thought that all such references were signs of my immaturity, although I was supposed to understand the atavistic attachment all these young English immigrant people had to the inferior drawing and stories to be found in their flimsy comic books called *The Beano* and *The Corker*.

So now she sat up and buttoned her blouse. She had a red circle on each cheek, and bits of dried leaf in her hair.

WILL AND I were in the little darkroom his father had helped us make under the stairs in his basement. This was before we bought our black plastic developer gizmo, so Will was holding both ends of the 127 film strip and pulling it back and forth through the tray, first the developer, then the stopper, then the fixer.

"Amsterdam," I said.

"Berlin," he replied.

"Oh yeah? Cardiff."

"Hmm. Dresden."

Pause.

"Edinburgh."

"Frankfurt."

"You can't just do German cities."

"No rule against it. Frankfurt."

"Geneva."

"Hamburg."

"I'm tellin' ya, Lieutenant —"

"Dum de dum de dum."

"Okay. Inverness."

"Jerusalem."

"Hah!"

"Or Jungfrau."

"Oh no, you don't."

"You could look it up."

"Don't think I won't. Köln. Ha ha."

"Leipzig. Tra la la la la."

"Munich."

"Shit!"

"Sorry."

"No, I mean I just got fixer all over my shirt. Nuremberg."

"Odense."

"Paris."

"That's not in Germany."

"So what? Who cares? Piffle. Paris, ah Paris. *Défense de stationner.*"

" Querétero."

"That is not in Europe, Cap'n."

"So what? I am well-travelled. *Quelquechose.*"

"I am playing this game under protest. Rotterdam."

"Stuttgart."

To tell the truth, there had been a not inconsiderable pause before that German city's name was pronounced. Now there was a more prolonged silence, during which we turned off the red light and opened the curtains and stepped out to the main basement, where Will clothespegged the dripping strip of film to a line we had running at face level a safe distance from the furnace.

"Trieste," Will finally said, a cheese-eating grin on his face. Now we could, if we wanted to, see one another's faces as we strode through the upper case alphabet.

"Uppsala," I replied, after an even longer pause. Now we

were carefully pouring the chemicals back into their dark brown jugs.

"Versailles. I have all of *la belle France* at my disposal."

"I will challenge your linguistic advantage with my courage and intensely-guarded work ethic," I replied, paper-towelling a little mistake on the plywood table. "Warsaw," I added.

"I, of course, spell that with a Vee," said my chum. "However, I will let your unilingualism go for the moment. Xenophiles."

"Wait a dad-gummed minute," I expostulated. "You always use Xenophiles. It doesn't matter whether we are doing cities or authors or sports heroes or movie stars. You always use Xenophiles. I don't think there even is any Xenophiles, in any category."

"Well, ask yourself," said Will, washing his hands with a big brown chunk of carbolic soap at the sink, "— if you are always going to start with the A, in a cheesy attempt to trap me into X and Z, shouldn't I get to pull out my secret Greek weapon?"

"I will let it go this time, but only because of your spirited and logical defence. Yalta."

"Zürich, which I insist on spelling with those two little dots over the you or the eye, whichever."

"Congratulations. We are done," I said, heading up the stairs toward baloney and white bread.

"And once again I am champion."

"How so? We got thirteen apiece, if my grade ten arithmetic has not deserted me."

"It works like boxing. Whoever wins the most recent bout is the champion. I am the champion of Zed."

The white bread was open on the oilskin tablecloth. The baloney lay nearby. Will approached with a jar of bright yellow mustard. Life was good.

I HAD MEANT to broach the topic of Jeanette with Will, but European capitals got in the way. I would talk about Wendy in a general way, bit by bit as Will and I hiked a hill or took empty beer bottles to the depot. But I didn't see how I could introduce the topic of Miss Verge. Will and I were boys, so we did not have long conversations about our private lives, our parents, and our high school loves. We were more likely to act out fictional romances, as in our comic public devotion to Dianne, the lifeguard at the pool I cleaned. She was from the Coast, and about four years older than us. We swooned and swore noble oaths. We called upon the muse of love. She smiled at us as she smiled at anyone else.

I don't recall getting an actual erection about Dianne. I can't speak for Will. I think he was the champion pudding pounder of the South Okanagan Valley. Dianne was not our only fictional damsel. We sometimes proposed to the two waitresses in the Oliver Cafe. We demanded that one of the tellers in the Bank of Commerce give us a guerdon to carry into battle. We did not carry wooden swords at our sides any more, not since grade eight, but we insisted on pageantry.

Looking back on my relationships or would-be relationships with girls and women, I have to admit that I tended toward the fantastical, looking as I seemed to be for a chance to rescue a damsel in distress rather than negotiate emotions with an equal. If you had asked me I would have said that dragons had never existed save in the fancy, but still I conjured myself as Saint George rather than Georgie Porgie. I did tend later in life to kiss girls and then make them cry. They would cry out of frustration and thwarted hope. And I often did run away like young Master Porgie.

Less than a decade after the events described here I let a young woman lead her father to believe that I was the father of the foetus he was going to have aborted for her. I didn't even ask why she wanted such a thing. I just loved her, and felt pretty good in a stomach-hurting way to be able to sacrifice myself in some high-minded way for her need. In return, she let me get Wendy out of my system.

It took me years to get from one lily pad to the next.

I wasn't in love with Jeanette, not as far as I knew. I just hated it that the world was not giving her the protection and happiness that was her due. I felt bad for her and on behalf of the world that was not her, and I was curious about her life. I had no clue that I was staking out a kind of liberal's position. Right and wrong were not so thoroughly interleaved in my life as they would become. Remember — I was never going to smoke and drink and all that.

I don't know — I could go a day or two without saying anything except those necessary things at the dinner table or going-to-bed time, but I wanted to hear Jeanette say something, I wanted her to talk about her life hidden behind the weeping willow and stuck this side of the swift silent river in the tulies. She would often walk all the way from the bridge down to Sawmill Road and all the way along Sawmill Road to her place without saying a thing to me. I would sometimes babble to make up for the silence. I would sometimes determine to keep silent myself, thus embarrassing her into speech. It didn't work; she was the silence in the middle of the forest, not that I ever used eastern book words like "forest" in any other circumstance, but there she was, a small gap in the universe. I had to make her say something. I took it as a personal challenge.

"What's the capital of Denmark?" I would say.

Nothing. She didn't care whether I thought she was smart or not.

"I'll give you twenty-five cents for a syllable," I'd say.

Silence. I thought about raising the price, but I had caught a silent notion that the money angle was a little crude.

"I can't remember. What house are you in?"

I don't think they do it any more, but when I was a kid, before cell phones and car-rides to school, the schools would arrange all the students into four houses, so that we could practise loyalty and compete in athletics and spelling and so on. I was in Saturn house, and glad of it, because Saturn was my favourite planet. Most kids liked Mars. Well, most kids also liked the Yankees.

I don't think that Jeanette ever heard of the Yankees or Joe DiMaggio. I don't think she would recognize Randolph Scott's courageous face. If I pronounced the name of Ray Bradbury she would probably not know whom I was talking about. It bothered me that I did not know what she spent her non-school time thinking about.

"What's your favourite comic strip?" I asked.

She didn't answer, either because she disdained to speak about such a topic, or did not read any comic strips at all. I found that sort of thing hard to believe or handle. It would bother me all my life that a woman I was interested in did not know how bad the Chicago Cubs were and how much one was called upon to shed fondness upon them.

And what did girls do while we boys were listening to "Red Ryder" or "Jack Armstrong the All-American Boy" on the radio? Or did the other boys listen to these programs, and "The Cisco Kid" and "Superman" before bedtime? I was in my loneness by the radio, making miniature movie houses out of glued-together comic strips. Or had I stopped listening to that stuff by the age of fourteen? Was I already a Hit Parade boy?

We started our walk from the bridge once again, and it seemed to me as if she was expecting me now, was comfortable with my silent or nosy attention.

"What's your favourite flavour of jelly bean?" I asked.

She did not answer, but the impatient look she gave me had

a trace of a grin in it. I skipped over to her left side so I could shield her from the traffic, as a swain should do. Traffic included tractors hauling wagons full of tree props made out of lodgepole pines that we called jackpines. Once I got to her left side I saw that her left eye was swollen almost shut and that the swelling was purple and yellow. I had not noticed at school, though now I remembered that in English class she had sat not in her usual seat but in the farthest back seat next to the window on her left. Mr. Hopkins must have noticed, and let her move there.

Now I really had questions to ask her.

"Lime," she said.

"What?"

"I like the lime ones. I hate it when you throw a green jelly bean in your mouth and it turns out to be spearmint." (What a trivial conversation to report or reconstruct in an autobiography, but I think that any reader can see the point).

It's normal to see a bad eye on a school boy. I have had my share. But a bad eye on a girl is a little scary, or at least it was back then. A black eye does not come from falling down, and hardly ever from a door. You hated to think of where it could have come from.

"Do you —?" I started.

"No, Nimrod."

She stepped behind me and over to my left.

I LIKED MAY and June all right. Summer was in, the blossoms had been replaced by little nubs of cherries and apples, and the pool was open. The pool was a swamp of sex for Oliver teens, or was that just me? No, I remember a lot of accidental rubbing up against in the pool. I remember lots of underwater swimming. I had time to think about these things while using the big brush to shove the green sludge down the slope of the empty pool, the sun high in the sky and throwing its rays down at my bare head.

There was a pretty good reason for my not liking this time of year, though. School was fast coming to an end for the year, and that meant that instead of sitting there learning neat stuff, I would be working in an orchard or the packing house. There was talk that I would spend this summer at the orchard up in Naramata where my Uncle Jerry was Foreman, a position of responsibility known in the local vernacular and the cowboy books I was reading as "Ramrod". That would mean the only time I could see Wendy would be on the weekends that I could come down to Oliver. And those weekends would arrive only if things slowed down in the orchard. When the cherries all got ripe at once, for example, we would be picking them at eight o'clock on Sunday morning.

The previous summer I had spent the month of August up there, staying in a little picker's cabin by night, every muscle in my thin body aching its way into sleep, and then in the daytime, picking peaches under a 100-degree sun, peach fuzz in the sweat at every joint of my body. I learned to wear a long-sleeved shirt in the intense heat, just to keep the fuzz off as much as possible, the collar done up, by every instinct the wrong thing to do. I love to eat peaches, but picking them was the worst job in the orchard.

"I have sensitive skin," I told my mother.

"You are just an overly sensitive boy," she said.

The end of school would also mean that I could no longer hook up with Jeanette at the bridge, and if I was going to be exiled to Naramata, I would probably not see her at all. It would not be a good idea to cut into my Wendy-seeing hours to pursue Jeanette every second weekend.

And just when my detectiving was getting into gear. Thank

goodness the teachers were backing off on homework, and thank goodness I didn't have any final exams to write. Because now I needed to step up my surveillance. Another silent walk from the bridge down to the river would not do it. I needed to see what Jeanette did at night. Or at least on the nights when I was not setting pins. I would have to catch up with Red Ryder and the Lone Ranger later. They were just about getting ready to go into summer reruns, anyway.

You see how all my values were sort of on a horizontal board, equally removed from the ground. If you saw a fourteen- or fifteen-year-old girl with a big swollen eye, what would you do? Would you ask your parents for advice, or would you talk to a teacher, or would you try to contact her parent? What a thought. All I could think of doing was sleuthing. I didn't imagine that there might be danger.

But as I walked her home from the bridge, this time she did deign to speak to me.

"Why don't you go and walk Bedelia Glottenschnaubel home?" she enquired.

"There is no such person, that's why."

"You swore up and down that there was. You told me she always has a piece of pie in her lunch. You told me her father was an aviator in prewar Germany. You said that she had muscular shoulders."

"I was trying to make you jealous," I said, pleased as hell that we had a conversation going.

"Do you think this is a conversation, Bowering?"

"One of my favourite, so far," I replied, trying to get a look at her eye. It was open now, but there were still shades of purple around it. Lilac, maybe.

"You have a brain that is deteriorating," said Jeanette, and stepped up our pace.

"I told Bedelia Glottenschnaubel that you were paying me to walk you home."

"If I had ten cents I would pay you to stay off this road."

That was it. She did not say another word all the way to her unpainted bungalow. I asked her who her favourite character from the Bible was. No answer. I said I would put her down for Noah. Silence.

I believed that she did not have ten cents. When I came to spy on her house that night I put a dollar bill on the windowsill of her room and put a rock on the dollar bill.

Then I hunkered down in the tall grass between her place and the river. There had been an unusually deep snow pack in the mountains the previous winter, so the river was high, and it was going by pretty fast, greenish brown with little swirls on the surface. This was the river that my mother told me I was never to enter. The best young swimmer in town had drowned in it the year before, after he fell from a chair he had been sitting in underwater. I never found out why he might have been doing that. Last winter Tuc-el-Nuit Lake had frozen over, and the best young skater in town had gone through the ice in a patch of warm current and drowned. I had skated a little on the lake that winter, Will and I desperately trying to kick snow onto the yellow areas we had made while trying to spell our names, Joan Roberts, otherwise known as the Student Body, leaving her house and heading in our usually friendly direction.

I was hunkered closer to the river than I would have liked, because some of the grass was growing right on up out of the water. I was a good swimmer, but I liked swimming in the pool or Tuc-el-Nuit Lake. I had never even been in the swimming hole where the river passed north of the train station.

There was no use hunkering in front of the house. There weren't even any lights in the front part of the house. People in

Oliver spent very little time in that part of the house, and you always knew that if anyone came to your front door it was probably a Jehovah's Witness couple or someone with a vacuum cleaner. Most people ate meals in their kitchen, and if they had a party most people hung around the kitchen and the back porch. I always did my homework or wrote my baseball stories at the kitchen table, and later in the evening my parents would play cards there, rolling cigarettes and drinking coffee.

From where I squatted I had a good view of the MacArthurs' kitchen, and there was Jeanette at the table. She was not doing homework or reading a book. I could hear the kitchen radio, but I could not figure out what kind of music she was hearing. She was sitting with her head bent as it was when she walked. I stood up to get a better look, and felt a thin tree branch across my eyes. When I could use them again I saw what she was doing there at the kitchen table. She had a light bulb stuffed inside a sock, and she was darning a heel. My grandmother had taught me how to do that, but she had a smooth wooden thing she called a duck to stick inside the sock. I did darn a few socks, but hadn't done so lately, though almost all my socks had holes in the front and the back.

So I watched her listening to music and darning socks. She did not bob her head to the tunes, nor use her hands for anything but the sock repairs, and I'd bet that she was not tapping her foot. I took note of all these things, but was I learning anything? As usual, she was alone. In fact, I had never seen anyone but her in that house. Really, it was not possible that she lived alone, was it? Was that why she had hardly any groceries and seldom any lunch?

I had had supper five hours before. Like most people in Oliver, we sat down to eat at five p.m., and we called it supper. Only after years of big city sophistication would I learn to call it dinner and wait till at least seven to start eating it. So here I was at ten p.m., hunkered in the dark, long wet grass against my pants. At ten p.m. in most parts of Canada around this time, it wasn't quite dark yet, but it gets dark earlier in Oliver because of the close mountains on the west side of the valley. There was an effect in July and August that I just loved. If you were on a hillside in the dark of night you could put your hand on a rockface and feel the heat it had been absorbing all day in the desert sun.

But here I was with my ass just out of the water, watching a drab girl darning someone's sock. I hoped that it was hers but I doubted it. I could just catch a hint of the radio's music, but more and more I became aware of the frog population. First I could hear a few individuals, their voices pitched slightly differently, but eventually I heard an *a cappella* chorus, and was sorely tempted to join in. Once in a while the chorus would cease suddenly, and I imagined a crocodile breaking the green-brown surface.

It was during one of those sudden gaps that I heard a sound that I was familiar with because of my rifle range experience with the Royal Canadian Air Cadet flight that I belonged to.

It was the sound of a bolt-action rifle placing a round of ammunition into the chamber at the behest of a human hand. The ammunition I had experience with was the .22 long. My ears did not tell me with certainty what calibre this one was, but I knew that it was not any other sound.

I will give my young self credit for this: I did not wet my pants. But I did not turn my head, either. I just waited. Then a male voice spoke, and I could not tell from what direction it came, only that it was no louder than it needed to be.

"Get the fuck home."

I stood up and began walking. I did not look behind me at all.

When I got into our house, as quietly as possible, my mother enquired of me the state of my homework.

"One," I said, "we don't have any homework this time of year. Two," I said, "when I do have homework, I do my French home-work in Math class, my Math homework in Social Studies class, and so on, ad nosy yum."

"Perhaps," was my mother's spoken opinion, "you would have more dramatic success with your grades if you did your homework at home, and paid more attention in class."

"They don't go fast enough in class, Mom."

I was glad to have this conversation, though I distinctly remembered having had it on an earlier occasion, because it enabled me to replace terror with cleverness.

"Keep your hands off the apple pie," my mother exhorted me. "It is for the bridge club tomorrow."

"Mom," I said. "Please teach me to play bridge."

"I will gladly push you *off* a bridge," announced my sister, who came into the kitchen at this moment. Then she went into the Norge refrigerator and got herself some vegetable. I once saw her standing on the front lawn, a white onion in one hand and a salt shaker in the other.

"If I saw you coming, I'd gladly jump off," was the acme of my wit this strange night.

CHAPTER 11

FOR THE PAST couple of years I had been eating a lot of Nabisco Shredded Wheat, which was all right with my parents, because it was one of the cheapest no-nonsense breakfast and bedtime cereals around. I don't remember what a box was worth when I was a teenager, but earlier, when I was in grade one and living in Greenwood, BC, it was twelve cents a box, rising to fifteen cents toward the end of the war. We usually had shredded wheat, bran flakes, corn flakes, and puffed wheat in the house.

My father, by the way, had the oddest way of eating shredded wheat. He would put one or two of the rectangular biscuits in a bowl, crack them open down the middle of their length, then pour boiling water on them to soften them, pour the water out of the bowl, and then lay brown sugar in the now sodden cracks. My father did not like milk. I thought that he was a peculiar man, and wondered about what I imagined to be his warped childhood, because he did not like milk or tomatoes, but he did like the New York Giants.

Nabisco Shredded Wheat in those days came in a rectangular

box in which were laid twelve wheat biscuits, three to a tier. That meant that there were three rectangular pieces of light cardboard in the box to separate the tiers. These separators were my reason for eating so much shredded wheat. I mean though I now do like shredded wheat, I was not all that crazy about it in those days. The box had a picture of the Niagara Falls on one end, one of the hundreds of reminders we were constantly given that all the important stuff happens way back in Ontario and Quebec.

It also happened that the linen letter writing paper my father used came in small sheets that were just a little longer and just a littler wider than the Shredded Wheat dividers. Let's say that the dividers were just under eight inches long and just under five inches wide. The writing paper was eight inches by five-and-a-half. If you have a hunch about what is coming, you may have been a kid like me.

My other equipment included an indelible ink pen, a pair of scissors, a window, some school glue, comic books, and the daily and weekly comics. Now, it happens that the artists who made comic strips were influenced by the movie people, so that once per strip they would make a close-up of a character's head. These close-ups were my target. I would go to the window, which in the South Okanagan Valley always looks out on a sunny day, or at least does so in the daytime, and trace one of those close-ups onto a piece of the linen letter writing paper. Each piece of paper would get five faces, and they always had to be from five different cartoons. One piece of paper, for example, might bear the faces of Gravel Gertie, Hotshot Charlie, Mark Trail, Scarlett O'Neill, and The Joker.

Once I had got five faces on a sheet of paper I would place the paper on a Shredded Wheat divider, snip the corners, bend the paper carefully around the divider and glue the edge to the back of the cardboard. I would make one of these cards every second week or so. I wound up with a pile, because the supply of comic characters was just about endless, and Nabisco was not about to stop making Shredded Wheat. It's a good thing that I started as early as I did — a few years later Nabisco started wrapping the individual biscuits and did away with the dividers.

I sure wish that I had those home-made collectibles now. Like a lot of things, they disappeared when my mother went on a neatness binge. I'd love to see whether I made a card featuring Joe Palooka, Skeezix, Goofy, Mary Marvel, and Hairless Joe.

The reason for my mentioning these cards, other than for reasons of my goopy sentimentality, is that on the last Saturday before the end of school in grade ten I walked the two long blocks down the hill and across the street to The Food Basket for a couple boxes of Shredded Wheat. And who should I run into in the store but Miss Verge, who followed me at the check-out with an enormous pile of groceries. Naturally we fell into a conversation, though I could feel a blush on my cheeks and for all I knew right down to my waist.

"Are you excited about the last week of school?"

"Ah, I guess so. But I kind of like school. Don't tell anyone."

"Do you have a job?"

"I think I'll be working at my uncle's orchard starting a week from now."

And so on. We talked and talked until her groceries were all in bags and paid for. There were about six bags of groceries, and this was back when the bags were paper and the packers filled them up.

"Would you do me a favour and help me get these upstairs?" she asked.

And I wondered for about a second and a half what she would have done if I hadn't come by. I think now that she probably had an arrangement with the store to help her get her stuff upstairs.

She lived right over the store, after all.

So once again I followed her up the long flight of stairs. With four of her bags in front of me I couldn't see much. She carried the other two bags and my little bag of cereal boxes. She had to put the three bags on the floor while she saw to opening her apartment door. It was not locked. I didn't know anyone who locked their doors in those days. But she took her time putting those bags on the floor in front of her feet, and in the dim light I could see her simple blouse fall open at the top, and also see a high percentage of her breasts. Wonderful globes they were, the breasts — tits — of a woman who was not really chubby but stocky. I really wanted to see them more, and I knew that it was out of the question, but I wanted to hold one in my hand. I did like Wendy's sweet young breasts, but can you imagine, I asked myself, holding one tit in two hands?

Miss Verge took her time standing up, and while she did she looked at me with her brown eyes wide open. Then she opened the door, bent swiftly this time to gather up the bags, and walked through and into her little kitchen. I followed, and as I did I heard a strong wind roaring through the trees inside my head. It was two in the afternoon in mid-June in the South Okanagan Valley. There were some open windows in the front and back of the apartment, but it was still pretty warm in there. That may have explained the fact that I was sweating at my hairline.

"You're nice and tall. You can help me put some of these things away," said Miss Verge.

To illustrate the necessity of such a thing, she stood on her tip-toes to attempt putting a loaf of bread on the top shelf, something she could never reach without a stool or a little ladder. When she did this her skirt rose up the backs of her muscular legs, up high, I mean, and I could see just a bit of white cotton, it probably was. Why, I wondered, would anyone keep the bread on the top shelf?

Her blouse had become untucked at the waist. I felt a tremor of fear. Should I get my Shredded Wheat and run for the door or should I see that the latter was locked?

"Here, you do it," she said.

And we started putting all the groceries away. Of course I could only guess where to put things. She also ate Grape Nuts Flakes, I noted. We kept bumping into each other, and the third time we did this she giggled a little. The next time I exaggeratedly reeled and gasped. We giggled and smiled and put away all the groceries. When we had finished we were both sweating at the hairline.

"Thank you, young man," she said, and she put her arms around me and gave me a hug. I could smell something like roses in her hair. I could feel her breasts against my midsection. I wondered whether she could feel my thickening cock that was now caught between my thigh and somewhere higher on her. My heart was beating as if it would come out through my chest. I began to wonder whether I had really come downtown for Shredded Wheat. Of course I had.

"I can hear your heart beating," whispered Miss Verge, but she did not take her arms from around me.

I tried to say something witty. Then I just tried to say something. I managed a little breath and a catch in my throat. I was fifteen years old and covered with sweat.

What was I supposed to do — tear myself loose and bolt for the door, my pants sticking out in front of me? I found that I had my arms around Miss Verge's shoulders, and I was holding on. I held a little tighter, in case I was in danger of falling off a cliff. I was so afraid of falling off cliffs that I would often climb a hillside just so that I could find one, a rockface back of the high school, for example. Then I would stand back from the edge. That night I would remember the cliff edge and know that what I was really afraid of was a kind of fascination, that I might throw myself off. Where you can't decide anything.

I don't exactly remember how this happened, but now I was standing with my back to the kitchen wall and Miss Verge was leaning on me a little. Then she leaned back without taking a step away, and the two top buttons of her white shirt were undone.

"Look at my eyes," she said.

I looked into her eyes and knew that I was supposed to keep doing so, and I did not look away from them when I felt her hands at the front of my pants. I think that my legs were shaking, but I stood and looked into her eyes. I didn't know what to do with my hands, those hands that had picked thousands of peaches and pears. I wanted to hold one of Miss Verge's large breasts, but I did not know whether I was supposed to.

Then my corduroy pants were open. My cock was all tangled in my underwear and I wanted to get it loose, but she batted my hand away and took care of it herself. Now she had my cock out in the air. I looked into her eyes and they looked back at me, offering a lot of language, more language than I had heard all day. She looked at me with her large round beautiful eyes, and I felt her fingers wrap around my cock, and then she moved her hand. I could not see anything, of course, but I knew that my cock was pointed almost straight up, and she was holding it in one hand while she cupped my nuts with the other.

I was alarmed, or course. No woman or girl had ever held my cock, except in my imagination while I breathed in bed. I was alarmed and I was nearly passing out for want of oxygen. I was looking straight into her eyes, but I could see the wide smile on her face. I really really wanted to stick my cock in somewhere, but I did not want her to stop moving her grip.

And then I felt that familiar rush, familiar but a hundred times more urgent, that furious spring from deep as it coursed up and then just about all over everywhere, or so it felt. She continued to pump as I spurted again, so thankful, so frightened. I looked into her eyes and then she closed them, moving her fingers more gently now, milking the last of me, then leaning forward and holding me again.

Eventually we disengaged. I felt sperm going cold on my skin. It was, as I had felt, everywhere else too, on my clothes and on hers. Her hand was covered with sperm. She helped me do up my pants before she wiped her hands on her shirt, which was totally unbuttoned now. Her bra was edged with lace and it was translucent. I could see that she had large dark nipples, totally unlike Wendy's small pink ones. Miss Verge saw me staring at them.

"Next time," she said.

"Next?" I could not construct a whole sentence.

She handed me a tissue that had been part of her grocery shopping, and I cleaned my shirt tail and cords as best I could.

At the top of the stairs she gave me a kiss and pressed her breast against me. Then she handed me my bag with two boxes of Shredded Wheat in it. It was all I could do to get down the stairs without falling.

"Holy Jesus" were the words I heard inside my head, but no image of the Saviour accompanied them.

∽

ON THE WAY home I picked up a bit of dirt and rubbed it into the stains. I figured that my mother would be so used to my dirty clothes that she wouldn't have a clue. In fact I wore my shirt and cords till supper time, when I changed into my pyjamas and ratty old robe.

"Are you planning on going to bed right after you've washed the dishes?" asked my unsuspicious mom.

"It never hurts to get a head start on bedtime," I said cheerily.

As it turned out I was pyjama boy out in the yard before dark, gathering chopped wood for the little kitchen stove and sawdust for the hopper. Thank goodness, I thought, it was summer and I could forget about the furnace for three months.

It wasn't really light enough outside to trace comic book faces against the window, so I played a couple of contests in my home-made big league game. I did not care if the Dodgers lost. I kept thinking of Miss Verge's badminton hand.

⌐↶

NEXT MORNING IT was Sunday in the Okanagan, bright and blue, cars from outlying orchards gathered along streets near the churches, bells ringing here and there, my parents in jammies at the kitchen table. My sister had left the house early to do chores at the United Church. My little brothers were in the front yard, throwing things at each other.

Since I had quit going to Sunday school at the United Church a couple years back, I never did go to church service there, except on Mother's Day, though I still went to the Anglican Church sometimes with Wendy and all the English people. In the summer we would go to Evensong because Wendy's father got up early and worked in the orchard all day Sunday. The cherries were coming on strong now, and in a week they would be thinning apples. Naramata was about a week north of Oliver when it came to fruit, so I would be headed for my uncle's place next weekend.

I came to the breakfast table in disguise. I wore my father's old brown leather jacket with the little rips in it, a pair of his ancient work pants, his nubby boots with laces made of shorter laces, all different colours, and an oversize welder's cap with car tire marks on it that I had found on the pavement behind Sibby's garage. Before putting on the cap I had wet my hair down and combed it straight forward.

"I take it you have landed a job at the junkyard," my mother said.

My father didn't say anything after his one quick glance at my getup. He was reading an Erle Stanley Gardner novel condensed in the *Star Weekly*.

"I keep hearing about this junkyard," I said, helping myself to the Shredded Wheat, "but I have no idea where it might be."

"Well, I'm surprised," said my mother.

"I know where the dump is. You go up Fairview Road and look for signs of civilization."

Will and I went to the dump once in a while to look for neat stuff. It wasn't all that great. I found an old box camera there once, and we turned it into a primitive enlarger for our dark-room. But we had a better time at the site of Fairview, the mining town that had been up there on a hillside flat years before Oliver was begun in 1921. Fairview had featured a jail, which was still there because it had been made out of iron bars and timbers with spikes in them, and a lot of hotels. We did not know much about these hotels, but once in a while we would find a tall buttoned shoe that had been snapped around a woman's ankle at the end of the nineteenth century. I wish I had kept one of those shoes. We usually settled for unbroken medicine bottles. Once we found a cook stove scattered around the site. If you go up there now, you won't find anything. Not since the availability of metal detectors.

Usually Will and I settled for the end of the irrigation season to begin our investigations, when we would put on rubber boots and walk miles down the irrigation ditch, looking for stuff caught in the green slime. Once I found a necklace made of Dutch coins. Once I found a small pistol with the handgrips gone. Sometimes we took our bikes and went way down south in the ditch, past Wendy's place, to the abandoned cement works. You could always find stuff if you knew where to look. We were boy detectives. When the concrete ditch gave way to metal to pass a small road or ravine, there were eight-by-eight boards across the top. We had to get off our bikes and bend over and push our way through the gunk. Detectives could not always sit in darkened automobiles, smoking cigarettes and watching windows.

I decided to be a detective on Sawmill Road once more before going to Naramata to thin apples. This would be a daylight reconnaissance. I took my bike and went way around past the little airport, so I could approach Jeanette's place from the south rather than from town. I left my bike at the back of a loading platform and approached her house via the river bank. The water had receded a little, so now it was just a question of walking in mud and not falling on one's pratt. Call me Bullfrog Drummond.

Jeanette was in the back yard, trying to push a lawnmower through the long wet grass. I could not see any progress at all, just places where she had obviously pushed the metal-wheeled machine through the grass, flattening it a little, twisting it some. She was bent over, yanking at clots of wet grass that were jamming up the dull-looking blades. I could just make out that she did not have anything on under her shirt, a man's shirt, it looked to be, too big for her.

"What are you, a peeping Don?" she asked, angry with the frustration of her hopeless task.

"Tom."

"What?"

"It's peeping Tom. And no, that's not what I am."

I was not about to tell her that I thought of myself as a detective. I did not want her to drop the mower and go inside and slam the door.

"Here you go," she said, really fast.

She had unbuttoned the shirt. Now she held it wide open and counted.

"One, two, three."

And closed it and started to do up the buttons.

"Now, Tom, you can go to your next back yard."

She was not blushing. I am pretty sure that I was.

"That's not why I am here," I said. "Not that I —"

They were wonderful. It was over too soon. It had started too quickly.

She tried pushing the mower. It jammed immediately.

"Were you here one night last week?" she asked. "Skulking in the bulrushes?"

I decided not to deny it. I had to break through somehow. I was going to Naramata Sunday after the ball game.

"Someone came after me with a gun," I said.

She pulled at the clogged grass.

"How do you know it wasn't me?"

"A man's voice came out of the darkness."

"Oh, *came out of the darkness*!" It was a jeer. "You think this is a book? You think you're a character in a book?"

Actually, that's exactly what I sometimes did think. But I was not here for that kind of discussion.

"Okay, let me ask you a question. How did you get that black eye?"

"Let me give you an answer," she said. "It's none of your business."

What could I do? Just dropping all pose and telling her straight-out that I liked her for some reason, and wanted to see whether I could help her in some way was out of the question. That's not the way kids talked to each other. I wanted to hold her hand or put my arm around her shoulder. I picked up the heavy end of the lawnmower and started pulling twisted grass out of the mechanism.

"You will never cut this jungle with this rusty old thing," I said. "You need a scythe, or that other thing, the little one."

"Sickle."

"You need one of those."

"I don't think I could be trusted with one of those," she said, and she would not look at me.

"If I can find one, I'll come down and cut the tall grass. Then you can push that hopeless thing through what's left. I looked at the grass and saw a tin can with no label on it and a rusted fork. "I mean, I have to go to Naramata to work, but if I can wangle a day at home, or maybe after — I don't know. Maybe I should come tomorrow with our hedge shears."

Jeanette did not answer me. I was pulling at smaller and more difficult bits of twisted grass. I felt that I had to quit this and head for my bike. I searched through my head for some brilliant shard of inventiveness, something I could do to get us talking about whatever it was, the dark stuff. Maybe it was just that Jeanette MacArthur was poor and her father was poor and no one had ever seen her mother. Maybe it was none of my business. Of course it was none of my business. A lot of people would tell me that. But sometimes the book I thought I was a character in had a whiff of the Bible in it.

Our family was not rich. While my father and I were digging the septic tank out, we all had to shit and piss in a tall bucket with a toilet seat on it. For years and years the exterior of our house was tarpaper and laths. I was never going to get my own baseball glove unless I earned the money for it. But there were no black eyes in our house. We could put sugar on our Shredded Wheat.

"Don't tell anyone, ever," said Jeanette.

"What?"

"Don't ever tell anyone, no one, I opened my shirt."

"Holy Crow! No. No," was my measured reply.

"I'm going inside."

"Can I —?"

"No," she said. "No."

I rode my bike into town, and turned right before Main Street, so I would not see any adults I knew on the main drag, and while I was at it, I just went for a ride, through neighbourhood after neighbourhood. In my head I was seeing Jeanette MacArthur's bare chest. I would shake my head, but a block later there it would be again.

*T*HE PLAN WAS that my whole family would go up to Naramata early in the afternoon on Sunday, spend the afternoon
playing bridge, goofing with the dogs in the orchard, eating
devilled egg sandwiches, and so on. Then my family would head
home in the late afternoon and leave me to get a good night's
sleep in my picker's cabin.

So I went to church with Wendy on Sunday morning. I was
still a United Church boy in St. Edward's Anglican Church, or
maybe I was a Neo-Thomist. That's what Louis Rinehart called
me after a short discussion of religion one afternoon at the packing house. I didn't understand what he was talking about, but I
figured it had to do with my habit of touching trees and houses
and smelling books and newspapers.

Wendy and I sat together in the pew behind the pew that held
her father and mother and sister and grandmother. Her little
brothers were downstairs, being looked after by happy pious
Anglican mothers. When Wendy pulled the kneeling bench
down and knelt to pray, I did too, though a nagging voice inside
me said that this was edging on paganism or ritual.

When we put the bench back up and sat again I noticed that Wendy had moved right up against me, that I could feel her warmth. I looked down and saw that her cottony print dress skirt was bunched over one knee, and I could see some of her straight bare thigh. Out of the left corner of my left eye I could see her look down at this rumple, and I expected her to use a white-gloved hand to correct this little accident. Sure enough, she did lower a hand to her leg, but not to cover her knee. Instead, she pulled her skirt hem up just a little more. I think she did.

While a man's voice filled the concrete nave with a good sermon about something praiseworthy, I held my head down, hoping to look thoughtful to anyone behind me, but really to look at Wendy's bare leg. I had seen her bare leg often, while swimming, while sunbathing, while wrestling on the orchard floor. But I had never seen it in church!

I felt Wendy's hip nudge me. I really really really wanted to put my hand on her bare leg in church, but I did not dare. I wanted God to forgive me for the stiffness in my slacks. I really really really wished that we were somewhere else and alone. The next time we got up from praying, Wendy sat a little apart from me, and her skirt fell nicely over her knees.

Afterward, when I was saying good bye to the Love family in the parking lot, I thought that I'd better not give Wendy a kiss. I just said goodbye to everyone, and waited till their rackely-backely old Hillman Minx had disappeared down the dusty road toward Granny Love's house.

Then, of course, filled with guilt because it was the Lord's Day, I went home and changed out of my good clothes, and while I was at it, beat my meat. Right on Carl Furillo's face. That made me feel guilty too.

CARROLL AIKINS WAS one of those orchardists who liked to call his big property a fruit ranch. He was also a playwright and dreamer, and had built a theatre on his property. The tarpaper pickers' cabins on the Aikins fruit ranch came equipped with little woodstoves for heat and for cooking. In July you didn't worry much about heat, but you kept your door closed to keep the mosquitoes out in the evening. The other pickers, like Paddy the Irishman with white hair on his head and a pipe in his mouth, usually upside down, cooked breakfast in their cabins, but I joined my Uncle Gerry and Aunt Pam in their kitchen. I was always the last one there and the last one to slide his chair back and head for the orchard.

I had two alarm clocks set at six-thirty in my cabin. One of them I put on the floor beside my cot, and the other I put inside the woodstove, with the lid off. I would put on my boots and pants and head for the outhouse, then came back and wash my face with cold water at my sink before heading for the house. I loved the roof of that house. Unlike anything in Oliver that I knew of it had cedar shingles on the roof, and dry yellow-brown pine needles all over the cedar shingles. When a summer thunderstorm smashed into the Naramata bench overlooking Lake Okanagan, the dump of heavy rain would find holes in that roof, and Aunt Pam would go back and forth, finding the buckets that were full and replacing them with empty ones.

But on sunny evenings while the picking was slow, I would be at their windows, tracing comic book faces. I guess that I was in a nice transitional position. I was a member of the family, but I was also a working man. Uncle Gerry was the youngest sibling in my father's family, and Auntie Pam was an ex-army girl from the coast with an inexplicable British accent. Before they had any kids of their own, I was sometimes a surrogate son. I would stay at their place when I was a pre-teener, and there are photos of me dressed in Auntie Pam's army jacket and cap. The jacket came down to my toes. There was a picture of me getting a piggy-back from Auntie Pam.

Once in those early years I was having a bath in their bathtub, and Auntie Pam asked me at the closed door whether I needed her to wash my back. I think that she asked because she had no experience as a mother. It had been years since my own mother had washed my back. I must have been nine, because the war was just over, and Auntie Pam didn't dress up in her army stuff any more.

"Yes, please," is what I said, a little shocked at myself.

I honestly can't remember now, but I probably put my hands over my little pecker so she wouldn't accidentally see it. And she took a washcloth and some soap and scrubbed my back. Ever since that event I have thought that bathtubs, and indeed all manifestations of water and the human body, are erotic. Wouldn't you think so?

It was from that time on that I had a child's yearning for Auntie Pam. I still see in my mind's eye the moment in the Kelowna kitchen when Uncle Gerry came up from behind and put his sinewy arm around Auntie Pam and held one of her ample breasts in one hand and called her "Pum." Boy, I wanted to do that.

Wait, wait. It just occurred to me that that is your classic Freudian triangle, as in D.H. Lawrence and so on, except that it is supposed to be your father and your mother. Maybe I didn't have the nerve with my mother, or maybe I was too much of a Neo-Thomist to be a Freudian boy. Anyway, I was not Freudian enough to kill my uncle and marry my aunt. I liked Uncle Gerry, and I remembered hearing lots of stories from my grandmother about what an amusing boy he had been. But I still took sneaky looks at Auntie Pam whenever she was reaching up to put wet clothing on the line or across the table to wipe up a marmalade smear.

I never have been very Freudian. For one thing, it has only been in the past few years that I have allowed that I might have an unconscious or subconscious or whatever it is. For the first six decades of my life I denied having one, denied that there was such a thing. Remember when Jake Barnes said that he believed in God for other people such as the bullfighters? At my most tolerant I would agree that there was such a thing as the subconscious for the people that needed it.

Anyway, most of the time around Uncle Gerry and Aunt Pam's house I could restrain myself. I usually went up to my cabin five trees back up the hill around eight-thirty, to read a book. During the summer when I was fifteen I was a science fiction reader, having tapered off on westerns. I was also reading books by other writers I had seen mentioned in magazines and newspapers, such as Erskine Caldwell and James M. Cain. Down in the lakeside village of Naramata I had made friends with a guy in the drugstore, and he gave me science fiction magazines after he'd ripped their covers off for their refund. Sometimes my memory amazes me. I don't remember what magazine it was, but I read a special issue on Poul Anderson. I liked him all right. My favourite book of his turned out to be *The Snows of Ganymede*. It was also the last one I ever read, because I was a college boy by then, and had to read Pound's *Cantos* instead, or so I thought. I am still reading those. I read one this morning.

Sometimes, though, I would get into playing cards with my aunt and uncle. I did the dishes while Aunt Pam got the kids to bed, and then we sat down and played hearts or whist or whatever was going around that year. Uncle Gerry almost always won. He and Aunt Pam kept a can of tobacco on the table, and rolled cigarettes all night. Once in a while I would smoke a tailor-made in the orchard, but I never had one in the house.

Uncle Gerry and Aunt Pam got up at six in the morning, so

these card sessions never went all that late. Still, sometimes it would be really dark by the time I hiked up the slope between the trees. I could usually see light coming from around the blind in Paddy's cabin, but the others were almost always dark by ten-thirty at night. On these nights I would limit myself to ten pages. I usually carried my flashlight up to my cabin, and then lit my kerosene lamp. I got pretty good at that after a couple of weeks.

A year or so earlier I had decided to start keeping track of the books I read. I started right in on the one I had just finished. I was not even tempted, as far as I remember, to record the ones I had read up till that time. But I have kept track ever since. I gave them numbers, starting with 1, and then an abbreviation for the publisher (B meant Bantam Books, PL meant Popular Library, a mass market paperback reprint outfit that's long gone), then the title of the book, followed by a dash, and the name of the author. Above the dash I would write in another number — if this was my third novel by Leigh Brackett, for example, I would put a three above the dash. For a while, on the inside back cover of my first scribbler, a blue one, I kept track of the numbers of books from the various publishers — Pocket Books, Dell, Signet. If I read a clothbound book I wrote in G&D, because the first few were from Grosset & Dunlap. In my late teens I decided to credit the actual hardback publisher, so Farrar Strauss became FS, etc. Around the same time I started another feature. When I had read a tenth book by some author I would get a piece of paper, half of an eight-and-a-half by eleven sheet, and type the titles in the order in which I read them. These I would staple on top of each other inside the covers of the scribblers. I now have a drawer full of scribblers listing the books I have read since I was around fourteen.

Of course I read more popular and literary magazines and newspapers than I do books. I average only about a hundred books a year, and as you might expect, or as you might your-self experience, this is maddening, because any amortizer will tell you that you can't read all the books you want to read, never mind all the books you have in your house, before you die.

For a couple months in that summer between grade ten and grade eleven I had a secret *crise de conscience* regarding the sci-ence fiction magazines I was reading. I reasoned that they were, in size and structure, very much like an anthology of science fiction stories such as those published by Fawcett Gold Medal Books or Ace Books. I gave in to the part of me that argued for adding a few of these to my list, giving them the title of the lon-gest story in the issue. For anthologies I would write the word "Ed." above the dash, and put in the editor's name. For these ersatz anthologies I used the name of the magazine's editor.

That summer I read (B) *Valley of the Shadow* by Charles Marquis Warren and (S) *1984* by George Orwell, for example. In the fall I would write a book report on *1984* and once more be thoroughly chided for writing about science fiction instead of real literature.

That was by Mona Hodgson, my grade eleven English teacher. For a joke I used to pretend that she was my sexual fantasy. Later I found out that she lived a sad life, married to a bluster-ing drunkard who liked to pass himself off as a British military officer. But that's another story, one that is unlikely to get told.

I thought that *1984* was a terrific book, and as I read it I knew that I was being shoved a little from science fiction into some-thing a bit more scary. I suppose I did not get that point across in my book report.

Outside the kerosene-lit cabin in which I read the book was a dark orchard cooling down from the day's blast of sun. The soil out of which the grass and asparagus grew was largely clay. You had to go a long way away from that orchard when you opened the pages of that little English book.

SO THERE I was, living my two lives — the one in the orchard and the one in the books. I didn't know how to characterize my feeling at the time, but I wondered increasingly how people could choose not to read books — how they could settle for living just one life. Even today I am puzzled by this. When I go to the doctor's office I know that I am not going to get to see the doctor at the time indicated on my appointment card. So because I always carry a book, in fact I am pleased to have an excuse for just sitting there and reading. But I am surrounded by people who just sit there with their expressionless faces pointed in one direction, and I am reminded that except for a few things we do, we human beings are just dumb animals.

If this were an essay rather than a memoir, I might go on to maintain that the reading one does improves one's living in the other world. When I am in Berlin, for example, I wonder what is happening inside the head of those young tourists who have never read anything about Berlin.

I wish I had known more about the Aikins family, the people who owned the fruit ranch I was working on. Carroll Aikins came from a famous and wealthy family in Quebec, where various of his ancestors had been in John A. Macdonald's government, for example. He wrote a play that was performed in Britain and he published quite a lot of poetry as well as books about Buddhism and the like. He and his wife Katherine were members of the Theosophical Society, and opened the Home Theatre in 1920, where they produced and directed some of the most famous or controversial modern plays of the time. A few years later, when fruit prices dropped catastrophically, they had to close the theatre and give all their attention to keeping the orchard going.

A few years ago I went to a terrific used book store in Penticton and snaffled a first edition, first printing copy of the *Selected Writings of Gertrude Stein*, Random House, 1946. It has a perfect dust jacket, and on the inside, in blue fountain pen ink it says "K.F. Aikins — Naramata —."

There was an enormous house next to Uncle Gerry's house, a giant old-fashioned thing made of wood and windows, screens and chimneys. Once in a while I went inside to look around. It had furniture and bookshelves the likes of which I had only imagined. All the wood was dark and shiny. The kitchen was enormous, a few steps down, and walled in tiles. This was the Aikins house in the orchard, just a few rows of trees from the little Penticton road above it. But now the Aikinses, I heard, were living in a huge new futuristic house down on the shore of Lake Okanagan.

Once in a while I would see John Aikins, a lawyer who was also heir to the biggest fruit ranch on the east side of the lake. One side of his face was a purple birthmark. When I first saw it, I thought he might have been hit by lightning. He was handsome, just the same, and always wore the kind of clothes you saw on wealthy rural people in English movies. I would see him and Uncle Gerry standing under an apple tree and discussing, I supposed, the success of the crop.

There are so many things that can threaten a crop. If it's too cold for bees in April, billions of blossoms will open in vain. If the coddling moth multiplies exponentially, your apples are doomed. One of the greatest anxieties for an orchardist is rain and hail during cherry season. The old wisdom is that in the south Okanagan Valley it rains twice a year — once in cherry season and once for the Labour Day weekend. If it rains when the cherries are a few days from picking, the water will gather around the stems from where the fruit absorbs it, and the next day's hot sun will split the big fat cherries. Hail will cut the cherries to pieces and do damage to the apricots, next in line.

People on the prairies like to boast about the size of the hailstones they have seen and the amount of topsoil they have seen passing overhead on the way out of the country. The biggest hail I have ever seen was falling on roofs and cars and trees on the bench overlooking Lake Okanagan at Naramata. I want to be careful about exaggerating here — they were no more than golf ball size. But they broke the windshield of Uncle Gerry's old Plymouth. They knocked shingles off the roof of his house, and henceforth Auntie Pam had to find more buckets to rotate around the house when it rained.

But that was last year. This year it was just rain. On my first Sunday morning up there, we skipped breakfast except for a big thermos of coffee and headed out for cherries, because the sky was full of low dark clouds that looked as if they might fall on us. I was standing on the top step of a wooden twenty-four foot ladder and using a long metal hook to bring the tallest branches down to where I could fill my bucket with black-red cherries, all the while getting wetter and wetter in the rain. I was not the fastest picker in the valley, and a wooden ladder is heavy and gets slippery in the rain, and thunder and lightning make for an unfriendly environment when it rumbles and flashes above the highest trees in orcharddom.

Uncle Gerry was up in the Giraffe, because he was a prodigiously fast picker, and the Giraffe basket could go from branch to branch quickly while I was clambering down my ladder, moving it, and climbing reluctantly up again. My buddy Will's stepfather Ted Trump had invented the Trump Giraffe. You know it generically as a "cherry-picker." We didn't know that other people had been inventing the device in other parts of the world. It would be used for work on overhead power wires, parked airplanes, and apartment fires, but right now it was being used by a cursing cherry picker on a dark wet Sabbath morning.

The idea was to get as many cherries as possible into the storage shed before the storm put an end to dreams of bonanza. There were eight of us all together, wet males of many ages trying to look upward in the rain. The thunder went bang a little louder all the time. I tried to remember just what materials are excellent conductors of electricity. It had been four years since we had learned that at school. I wondered whether I were the only person here in this wet forest of cherry trees willing to abandon profit for a dry chair under a roof not far from a toaster.

The loud booms got closer and became more frequent. I sensed our altitude above the lake. The bucket of cherries I had hanging from a branch in front of my face had an inch of water in the bottom. I made a mental note to invent a cherry bucket with a circle of screen in the centre of the bottom.

Then there was a white crash. Then sound was removed from the world. From the top step of my twenty-four-foot ladder I saw Uncle Gerry lower the steel basket of his Giraffe and jump out of it before it had come to rest. I saw him waving his arm at me and then waving it at the others. I could see that his mouth was wide open in his wet face but there was no sound. My bucket was only half full but I got down my ladder as quickly as I could in the wetness. I poured my half bucket of cherries into my last lug of the morning, and then we put tarps over the gleaming lugs. It was time to slog up the muddy road to the house.

Uncle Gerry didn't have any boots on.

He pointed to the rubber tires of the Giraffe and silently shouted something. I agreed entirely, and followed his slippery barefoot steps up the road. Every big raindrop felt like a little fist.

Well, I didn't pee myself, I thought. But then with all this water, who would have noticed?

⚓

OF COURSE NEXT day the Okanagan sun came out and split the cherries. I have noticed in recent times that some orchardists hire a helicopter to come and hover over their cherry trees after a rain. It costs a lot to hire a helicopter, so a heavy cherry crop must be pretty valuable. I don't know how much the Aikinses lost to that lightning storm, but the cherries we picked for the rest of the week must have been sixty-five percent culls. I felt less guilty gobbling them. I always, though, spent a lot of time in the outhouse during cherry season, especially on the first day.

We picked like crazy all the week after that storm. I think Uncle Gerry half expected another day of thunder and lightning, but of course this was the South Okanagan. Each day the sun blazed harder. I got a sunburn even though I had been going around with no shirt on for a month. After I peeled I started tanning, and it was not long till my skin was almost as dark as my hair. We were never told about the deleterious effects of the sun's rays in those days, and maybe there weren't any. I never heard of anyone with skin cancer. We thought of sunshine as a cure for acne, arthritis, and allergies, and that was just the first letter of the alphabet.

And after a week of long days lifting ladders and climbing trees, the pain disappeared from my back and legs. I was tanned and fit. And I was making sixty cents an hour. Those cents were going to pile up and earn interest in my college fund bank account. Meanwhile I dropped by the playing fields down by the lake and sort of joined the Naramata Nomads junior baseball team. I had played one game for the Oliver juniors before heading north, so I told myself that I had just been involved in my first trade. I never told anyone else and it was not true, but it was a neat story that would slide effortlessly into the inaccurate memoir I was writing in my own head.

If work on the orchard was not too pressing, Uncle Gerry would let me go to Nomads games and practices. I would have to walk all the way down the path in the clay cliff ravine to the waterfront, and afterward I would have to hike all the way back up. But I had been a hiker for years. For the Nomads I was a reserve because they could not expect to see me every time they took the field, but I was technically available to fill in at any position, though so many guys wanted to pitch that I never got to take the mound. Before my trade I had gone one for four in Oliver. To tell you the truth, I don't remember what my average was in Naramata. I do remember our hats, though. They were black with an ordinary white N on them. You hardly ever see just an N on a baseball cap.

One time we had to wait an extra hour to get onto the field because there was a cricket game finishing up. We thought it was funny, this fey game played by Englishmen in white slacks. So we sat there and made juvenile jokes about the way the guy threw the ball and the way the runners held on to their bats. Eventually we got to mark our baselines and get onto the grass, and some of the cricket guys, all older than us, made cracks about our game. We didn't understand what they were saying.

We were all tanned, though, all the cricket players and all the baseball players. Our white outfits made our tanned skin look really good. A lot of the little kids and teenaged girls who watched us play were in bathing suits, the most common item of clothing in the valley. They were really tanned. Sometimes they would run into the lake for a minute and then come back, shining and shivering in the heat, their skinny legs all crooked under them.

Most of the other Nomads were lining up with local orchard

girls or with the girls from the church camp just down the lake. But I was in a kid's way engaged to Wendy Love. No Naramata fling for me.

⌒

MY FATHER HAD taken back his job writing the Oliver baseball stories for the *Chronicle* and the *Herald* now that I was away. There was no senior baseball in Naramata, and the paper was not interested in anything more than the final scores of the junior games, so I had no journalism to do that summer. Therefore, of course, I had more time for other kinds of writing. It would be another seven years before I started keeping my diary, so all I did was a little poetry and some stories that I thought were comical or maybe even satirical. Really, I wrote them just for Will to read. I knew that he would like them.

For example, I always changed the lyrics of popular songs. Sometimes I made up brilliant new verses, though more often I merely made obvious juvenile switches. Just this morning, for instance, I remembered singing "If I knew you were coming/ I'd have faked an ache." Well, it was not one of my favourites at the time. I wrote little stories about Sam Shovel: Private Eye, Ear, Nose, and Throat. It feels so confessional, revealing this jejune material now. Someone once told me that confession is good for the soul. I knew from that very second that he was full of it.

Luckily, I spent more time reading than writing. I was still so innocent — I could read a novel without considering what it had to teach me about writing a novel. When I read four hundred westerns in those years, I had no idea that I would many decades later write and publish a couple. Now I can tell you — a few years ago I read a western by one of my old favourite authors, and I really enjoyed it, got into it, and did not once stop to think that I could use something I found there. Today I picked up an old beat-up copy of Joseph Conrad's *Chance* and I hope that something like that happens again.

One night after supper and a game of cribbage with my uncle, I was kind of excited while I headed up to my cabin because I knew that I was going to finish reading *Trail Dust* by Bliss Lomax. I had thirty-five pages to go and a full kerosene lamp. I had snitched one of the cigarettes Aunt Pam had rolled, and my stomach was nicely full of mashed potatoes.

There was still a band of light in the western sky, and warmth coming off the clay earth. If I left the door open there would be enough light for me to ignite the lamp without using my flash-light. But as soon as I stepped in, the door closed as if by itself, but without slamming. Yes, the hair does feel as if it is rising on the back of your neck when something like that happens.

I reached blindly for the door, and a hand that seemed to be accustomed to the dark closed around my wrist. Is some-one robbing me or killing me or what, I wondered, of course. It was totally dark in my little room. The hand's fingers remained around my wrist.

"Stay still."

It was a whispered voice. I pulled my hand toward me a little. The hand held firm.

"Still."

It was a female whispered voice. I stayed still. There was a home-made cigarette in my free hand. I put it in my shirt pocket.

"All right. The chair is just to your left. Step sideways and sit down."

I didn't move. The hand levered my arm and I went sideways. I reached carefully with my free hand and sat down slowly. Then my other hand was free too.

"Just sit quietly and don't say anything."

My heart was going fast and high. Fear had been running from nerve to nerve all through my body. Now something else was starting to run beside the fear. The window blind was down, though I was sure that I had left it up when I went to work in the morning. Something slippery was against my face and then in my hands. It felt cool and warm and cool again. I knew it was something like silk, a silk shirt. I heard little bits of breathing, as if someone were doing an exercise. There was a skirt in my hands on my lap. What was I supposed to do? Hold onto everything? Put everything in a neat pile beside the chair? There was something else in my hands. I passed it from hand to hand. It was a bra. A pretty large one, by comparison with Wendy's. For a second I dared to guess that this was Auntie Pam. But hadn't she been in the living room when I left Uncle Gerry at the kitchen table?

"Who —?"

"Shhh. Just stay still and don't say anything," came the whisper.

Some light thing landed on my head and slid down me onto the floor somewhere. Then I heard steps on the linoleum floor of the cabin. She was walking in high heels on the floor, to my left, and then to my right.

"My eyes are adjusted to the darkness," she whispered. "I can see you. At least I can see the shape of you and a little of your face, George."

I knew the voice now, even the whispered voice. I knew who it was that had taken her clothes off in front of me, not for me to see but for herself to see herself doing it in front of the boy that could not see. Now a little line of faint light showed on either side of the blind. I peered but I could not see, only sense a darkness in the middle of the darkness.

"Take those heavy boots off," whispered the voice.

I was going to do that anyway, I reasoned, or did not reason.

I took off my boots and dawdled a little, lining them up against the wall as best I could in the dark.

"Now," whispered the voice I knew, "stand up."

I hope you realize that while these alarming occurrences did happen, the scraps of dialogue you find here could not be *verbatim*. In offering the dialogue I am trying to remember and present the spirit of the events. It will be as if I were writing something like a novel about actual events. In some instances I am pretty certain that these words are just what they were. For every occasion I am trying to be true to the intentions and observations of Jeanette, Wendy, and Miss Verge, as well as various of my relatives, etc.

I stood up. My eyes had now adjusted somewhat, and I could see a line of pale light down each side of the blind. There were two lines of faint light in the room, and once in a while one of them would cut across the naked figure in front of me. Naked, that is, except for the high heeled shoes I could hear on the floor. Naked, that is, except for the shoes and the stockings that would have to go with the shoes.

Standing up in the dark and keeping your balance is harder than it seems, and it certainly was this time, what with all there was to consider.

"Stay still," said the whisper, up close.

Her fingers moved around my short-sleeved shirt and found the top button. They undid that button, and then found it easy to go down from button to button, opening them as they went.

Holy Jesus, I thought, I should do something. I should say something. She seemed to have heard these words in my head.

"Stay very still," she said. Then she kissed my chest.

I heard the unmistakable sound of a knee cracking as she knelt down in front of me, her fingers helping her keep balance by hanging from my trouser tops. I shifted my feet as little as I could, to keep my own balance. Then her fingers were at my belt. Someone else's fingers are never as adroit as your own when it comes to undoing belts and buttons, but this was only the second time I had experienced this since the days long ago when my mother helped with mine. Back then I was eager to do it myself. This time I was becoming more and more willing to obey the injunctions I had heard about remaining still.

The belt was undone. The fingers were busy at the button and then the zipper. It had become very quiet inside the cabin, and I clearly heard the downward zip. In a thin line of light I could see part of a forehead turned upward to me. Those blue jeans were a little tight. But her hands guided them, and soon they were crumpled on the floor. Her hands showed my feet what to do, and I stepped out of both legs. I heard the belt buckle hit the floor beside us.

"Put your hand on my head."

"What? What?"

"So you won't fall over while I help you off with your socks."

I did as I was told, and when I did I could see a phantom of my white jockey shorts and as soon as I felt Miss Verge's hair under my hand, that which was contained by the jockey shorts rose, though I would have thought it impossible, even higher than it had been. This fact made it a little more difficult but no less interesting for Miss Verge to remove that last garment from my thin body. She had to reach inside and hold the item down as far as it would let her while pulling the waistband upward as far as the elastic would allow. When I silently offered to help, she pushed my hand away. Finally she got the jockey shorts loose and began pulling them down, releasing my thing, which then slapped against my belly.

Still on her knees, she held my testicles in one palm and wrapped the fingers of her other around my thing. Then, as I faintly made out her dark form she placed one medium-sized kiss on the very end of it.

Would you — I began to say inside my head.

"Not right now," she said out loud, and I heard that knee again as she stood up, using my now aching thing for leverage.

I had always thought of myself as a good boy, a good person, a kind of Christian if not actually noble, an individual who possessed the aim in life of making the world a better place in which to live. I had sexual desire, of course, being a male adolescent at the mercy of his chemical makeup. But I had always assigned stories of illicit sex to the guys who played hooky and stole cigarettes and failed their spelling tests. Now here I was, standing naked in a small room with a naked teacher from my own school, naked, at least, except for shoes and stockings. I vowed that no one would ever hear this story. There would be no jokes in the lavatory. I would not even tell Will about my adventure. I would not write it down anywhere. I was pretty sure that I was going to lose my virginity, as the quaint phrase had it. But this would not be an occasion for boasting or even self-ridicule, if it came to that.

As for the question of right and wrong? I had stopped using the word "sin" in my conversations with myself, but I did have rules, and they were commensurate with my ambitions to live life as a good person. Here, at this moment, I began to bargain. If, I asked myself, this is more a case of something being done to me than my trying to get something for myself, can we say that any fault accruing to my part will be minimized by the situation?

My eyes were as well adjusted to the darkness as they were going to get. This was all happening seven years before my first pair of eyeglasses, though I knew back then that my eyesight was a little fuzzy. Still, there was a little light coming in between the boards of the walls, some from the edge of the blind, and a little from a small circular hole in the roof. I could still hear and feel better than I could see, but when I looked down I could see my white jockeys in a puddle, as they say, on the linoleum.

Now I felt a hand on my buttock, very gently urging me toward the bed. It was more a cot than a bed, like something you would find in a barrack. It was just wide enough for one person and his book.

I remember actually thinking about whether I would get any reading done before sleeping this night. There I was, naked, suspended between alarm and anticipation, my heart beating whatever blood was not in my penis. I sat on the side of the bed, my bare feet on the linoleum.

"I shouldn't," I said.

"That's right. You are bad," she whispered, and lifted my feet onto the bed. I felt her weight, then, beside me and on top of me, and she ran one hand from my head down to my belly, around my cock, and then down to my feet, as if laying me out flat. I didn't know what to do with my hands. One arm was up around my head, and the other was by my side, between us. Then I felt her mouth on mine. It was a little open, and her lips and the tip of her tongue found their way around my mouth and my cheeks and chin, my ear, my mouth again. I still didn't know much about kissing, I realized then, and I let her tongue urge mine to look around inside her lips.

We were really too much human being for this little bed. I felt my left hip touch the plywood wall. But if I shifted so that I could lie on my side, my cock would be against Miss Verge. She nudged me, and I shifted. Her skin felt cool and firm against my cock. My left arm was beginning to ache because of its unnatural angle above my head, and I was wondering what to do with it when she reached for my hand and brought it to her breast. It too was cool and firm. I felt her nipple rise and harden between my fingers. I didn't know whether this phenomenon should put me off or delight me. Wendy's small breasts had tiny nipples at their centers.

This was so awkward. I began to wish that we had a double bed, or a haystack. I moved my left hand, feeling whatever I could, both large breasts, a shoulder, neck, breasts again. Miss Verge kissed me again, and it seemed that she meant to keep her mouth on mine forever, and while she kissed me she lifted her bent right leg over me and this caused something hot to press against the backs of the fingers on my trapped right hand. I pushed with my knuckles, and I knew what this was, though I could not believe it. I stuck my tongue halfway into the mouth that was sucking mine.

This time she nudged me and took my head in her two hands and directed my face to her wonderful chest. For a while I had my mouth and nose between them, then like a blind baby mammal I rummaged until I found a large erect nipple and slurped it. Is this all right? I asked myself. I'm not a baby, for god's sake, but listen to her.

"Ah," whispered Miss Verge. "Ah." And she had a hand on my head.

I felt her other hand push my left hand until it was over her hot centre. I let my fingers cup it, felt the suddenly permissible hair, till my middle finger encountered what would have been a gleam if I were seeing it. Do you know what I mean? A slick that made way, and my finger was inside, where it was wet and hot, a cunt, a teacher's cunt, holy god! Her hips and bum lifted to me, and I replied by sucking her nipple hard.

"Bite," she whispered.

I gently bit her, and her hand closed over the hand that was on her heat, and I put in a second finger.

Then she nudged me again, nudging her way under me, moving her legs apart and flexing them and lifting them behind me.

There I was, just as I had always imagined. What do I do now, I wondered. How do I? Then I felt her hand take me and put me where it was meant. It went in or I did, and I felt what I had always merely dreamed, and it was as if I had been there often. No one had to tell me that I should dig as if I were listening to jazz, and certainly Miss Verge helped me, there so fully in her flesh but dancing like a badminton player — I actually thought of that — and before long I did what I had so often done, but this time inside, where anyone wants to be, and I forgot who we both were for a moment.

You know what happened. We rested, listening to our breath inside the little tarpaper shack. I did not fall asleep and I did not have a cigarette. In a little while Miss Verge held my cock and it grew again, and she put it in, and this time she made a rapid high-pitched sound back in her throat, and I was afraid that my relatives or fellow workers would come running to rescue me, but all of a sudden I was put in mind of the rodeo I attended every summer, and then she collapsed, squeezed me tight, then fell back again, and this time I did drift off to sleep, with a frightened smile, I know, on my face.

I woke to a somewhat lighted room, alone in my tangled bed. I got up and went outside barefoot to pee in the orchard. A patina of early grey light made its way between the tree branches. I held my pecker in my hand and smiled as I made an arc of visible water into the tall grass.

CHAPTER 13

LATE IN JULY the Naramata Nomads travelled to Oliver for a double header. At the Aikins ranch we didn't grow that many apricots, and peach picking wouldn't get really hectic for a week or so, so Uncle Gerry gave me the go-ahead to make the trip. I think that he might have been giving me a break because I hadn't seen my family for three weeks. Once peach season really got going I'd for sure miss a few road games and maybe even the home ones. In the orchards, sunlight is an asset you don't squander.

The Nomads piled into the coaches' cars early Sunday morning, and engaged in noise and horseplay all thirty-seven miles to Oliver. We waved at people on orchard ladders along the route, and sang what we thought were questionable songs with the windows wide open. At nine in the morning, when we arrived, it was already over eighty degrees at the Oliver baseball park.

It was very strange to be a member of a visiting team at the Oliver ball park. I tried to look at the big irrigation siphon, the soaring cottonwood trees, and the wooden community hall as if I were a tourist or some other kind of outsider. It almost worked.

It was also the first time I had ever been in Oliver as a non-virgin, and I suppose that made some kind of difference too. It was easy to imagine myself being interviewed by a girl reporter for the Oliver *Chronicle*.

OC: How do you think you will feel, playing against your former teammates? Will it be an advantage, knowing them so well, especially their pitchers?

GB: I think the biggest challenge will be coming to bat in the top of the inning instead of the bottom. I look at the scoreboard out there, and I can't believe that we are going to be on the top half.

OC: What has it been like, playing for a new team after starring for the Elks all these years?

GB: Well, it was really less than one year, and I can't say I was a star. I'm now what you call a journeyman player. When my team needs a pinch hitter, I'm there for them. If they need someone to fill in as catcher in the late innings, I'll don the tools of ignorance.

OC: The what?

GB: Mask, chest protector, catcher's mitt. We call them the tools of ignorance in the trade.

OC: I don't get it. Are catchers ignorant? Who would want to be called ignorant?

GB: It's an expression. Third base is called the hot corner. We talk about having strength up the middle. If the pitcher throws the ball from way down near the ground he's called a submarine chucker. Your outfielders are called gardeners. The right fielder ought to have a rifle out there.

OC: Rifle?

GB: Look, if a hitter drives a liner through the shortstop, do you imagine a sea captain at the helm of an ocean-going vessel passing through the body of an infielder? I am talking baseball talk. Aren't you a newspaper reporter? Don't you ever read the sports pages of, say, the St. Louis *Post-Dispatch*?

OC: The what?

GB: The Cleveland *Plain Dealer*?

OC: The *Chronicle* sent me down to —

GB: The San Francisco *Chronicle*? That's a Pacific Coast League paper. We're talking the majors here.

OC: I don't understand why you are bugging me like this. I would think that you'd be glad to be covered by the *Chronicle*.

GB: To tell the truth, I'd rather be covered by you. But not after I have donned the tools of ignorance.

OC: Now, hold on —

GB: You are too good-looking to be a small town newspaper reporter. How old are you?

OC: I am twenty, which makes me about five years older than you.

GB: I have a *penchant* for older women.

OC: A what?

GB: You old babes make me horny.

OC: Please —

GB: Look. Come across or walk home.

OC: Really. I always walk home. And I wouldn't be getting into your car, if you were old enough to drive.

It hadn't taken me long to learn that you can't expect the usual adulation from the out-of-town press. Or that a ballplayer is without honour in his hometown.

We had a morning game at ten-thirty, and in order to accommodate the churchgoers, a second game was scheduled for two p.m. Wendy, I imagined, would be a churchgoer this day. Whether to expect her at the ballpark for the afternoon was an open question. I had not written to tell her about the game, and I didn't expect that she would have read about it in the paper.

Back in those days you did not make long distance telephone calls unless something terrible had happened. Even today, when I see that a long distance call is coming in I tighten up, wondering who has died.

Still, before my trade I had showed Wendy how to keep score. If the hitter flies out to left field, I told her, mark a 7 in the square. Don't mark it F7 unless the guy fouled out. Wendy was a smart girl, smarter than I in about five hundred ways, so she caught on fast, even though she was supposed to be a grass hockey and cricket girl. I had some hope that she would show up, and that she would keep score for me. Despite that fantasy interview, I was planning, of course, to cover the doubleheader for the *Chronicle*.

Our flannel uniforms were heavy and sweaty by the second inning of the morning game. Though I was not in the starting lineup, but coaching at first base, I was sweltering, whatever that is. It was a game marked by errors and wild pitches, so I was a wee bit disgusted. In the fifth inning, Jay Kinsella, our little second baseman got hit by a pitch right on his left foot. He tried to walk it off, but when the umpire reminded us that we had two games today, out he came, and I took his place on the bag at first. I made it as far as third, and later took part in what would have been a double play if our first baseman had been able to pluck my throw out of the dirt, and later still reached base on an error by Oliver's third baseman, Ritchie Schneider's little brother. But we still lost the game 14–10. I just looked it up.

The morning game was scheduled for only seven innings, thank goodness, but the afternoon game would go nine. I mean thank goodness because of the errors, not because of the heat. Between games we headed for the shade of the community centre and dug into the lunches we had brought. Our manager drove up to the Orchard Cafe and brought us back bottles of pop.

I can still see mine — a big dark brown bottle of Orange Crush. I
swirled the residue in the bottom before I opened it, because that
is what you did with Orange Crush. That was why you chose
Orange Crush — because no other pop had residue in it. When
they started selling Orange Crush in clear bottles with no rings
and no residue, I knew that the future would forever remain
inferior to the present. When rolling tobacco started coming in
cubes of cardboard instead of cans, I was confirmed in my belief,
though I never bought rolling tobacco.

⌐⌐

I STARTED AT second base in the second game because Jay had
taken his spikes off after the first game, and now he couldn't get
his left spike back on his swollen foot. Jay was the only other guy
on the team that wanted to know everything about baseball the
way I did. Most of the guys just had athletic ability and wanted
to play the game. They didn't learn the rules much and they certainly did not know who Rabbit Maranville was.

It was deucedly hot, as my grandfather would say and even
though the dugout was shady it was not cool. There was no
breeze. I was almost praying for the wind that would blow cotton
off the trees and make it look as if we were playing in a blizzard.
We had gobbled up the big sack of orange wedges before the
third inning, by which time we were trailing 4–0. Mr. Gludovatz
the plate umpire was wearing one of those big inflated chest pro-
tectors, and the back of his shirt was one massive sweat stain.
Sweat gathered in the creases at the back of his neck.

There was some shade in the old grey grandstand, and there
were maybe twenty people in the seats, some of them fanning
themselves with magazines, others undoing buttons. Wendy had
arrived with her little brother David, a kid I liked despite the
folklore that says your girlfriend's little brother is supposed to

be a pest. I had never given him a quarter to get lost. They were not in the grandstand, but in the little bank of open seats right behind our dugout. I didn't know about Wendy, but it was clear that David was cheering for us Nomads. In the first inning there were two Oliver guys on base and their best slugger up to bat. In his high-pitched little voice, David yelled encouragement to Morris Stoochnoff, our pitcher.

"Tip him over!"

"Shh!" his big sister suggested. I *think* that's what she said.

I was proud of him.

"Deck him!" I yelled from my second base position.

Of course we did not get out of that jam, and by the fifth inning we were down 6–0, and no one on our team had acquired a hit. Ordie Jones, their pitcher, had tossed a no-hitter against Summerland at the beginning of the season, and it was beginning to look as if he would get another one. I couldn't look at Wendy.

But I looked up at the sparse gathering in the grandstand, and there, with the red-headed art teacher, was Miss Verge. Teachers come out to watch school kids play ball? They were both wearing fairly long white shorts and white shirts and straw hats with wide brims. They were both wearing sandals and no socks. When an Oliver guy got on base they both clapped their hands. I tried not to look at them. But when I trotted toward our dugout after the third out we had been lucky to manage, Miss Verge waved to me, and, after a second, so did the red-headed art teacher. I gave the smallest wave of my glove hand that I could.

I saw several of the Oliver players looking at me and then at the teachers, and then back at me. When I came up to lead off in the top of the seventh, the catcher made a loud sucking noise.

That seemed to do the trick. Ordie Jones left a slow curve ball over the outside part of the plate and I had time to wait a bit and then hit it hard into right field. It landed inside the line and skipped the rest of the way foul. I have never been a dealer in speed of foot, but I chugged all the way to third base in my flannel and my too-tight shoes. Being as to how we were the visiting team, there was no collective display of patriotism in the crowd, but as I was standing on the bag with my hands on my hips and my chest heaving up and down I cast a glance at the teachers, and I saw Miss Verge clapping her hands. I looked over at Wendy, and while her little brother was waving his hands in the air, she seemed to be trying to untangle her hair where it met her glasses.

I had a look at Ordie. I knew that he was pissed off that he would lose his no-hitter to an underachiever such as me. He would not look at me, not even to check the runner before pitching to Bobby McBride. He knew that I was no great shakes on my feet, and he needed something right then.

I still hadn't caught my breath when Bobby hit a fly ball to centre, and I barely made it home ahead of the throw. It would be the only run we scored in the second game, and it would be the only triple I would hit until one rainy night in the Kozmik League in Vancouver twenty years later.

It was as hot as the ante-room to Hell, and we were sweaty and dirty, and there was no dressing room at the ballpark. I know that the senior ball teams that came to town always got showers at the swimming pool dressing room, but for some reason we were expected to ride all the way home to Naramata in our uniforms. At least we could change into running shoes and carry our spikes with our gloves. Most of us took off our heavy shirts, even the guys with skinny hairless chests like mine. I took mine off and left it along with my cap and glove and my father's old spikes in the trunk of the coach's car.

I scanned the seats and the grounds but saw no sign of the

teachers, and then went over to the bleachers to talk with Wendy and little David. I hinted to the latter that he might go and chase dragonflies, but he was a baseball-crazy little Canadian kid. He was all wound up. Wendy was kind of a sister and kind of a baby-sitter for this six-year-old boy with very short blond hair.

"That was the greatest hit I have seen in my whole life," David pronounced.

"It was ninety percent luck," I said.

Wendy looked just beautiful in a mid-summer unconventional alien British not quite finished way. She used her hand to wipe some sweat off my bare chest, and I just about jumped out of my moist skin.

"I thought you were going to have a home run," expostulated David.

"I thought you had seen me running before," I answered.

My coach was honking the horn of his car. It was time to head north, back to the clay cliffs over the lake. I hugged Wendy and gave her a pretty good kiss, all things considered, and told her how much I wished that I could stay in town overnight. I felt that way about my parents too. How odd it was to come to Oliver and not see my family. But I was a working stiff and a ballplayer. This is the life you get when they force you to grow up. I vowed to grow up in as few ways as it was humanly possible.

On the way up Highway 97 the coach found an ice cream garage and treated us all to Creamsicles even though we had dropped both ends of the doubleheader.

THE COACH LET me off AT the Aikins driveway, and I ducked the divebombing kingbird as I trudged dead tired to my cabin. When I turned my head to the left I thought for a second that I had seen someone stepping behind an apple tree. But that was always happening, wasn't it? I wondered who it was, and then I told myself it wasn't anyone.

Supper was usually at five on Sundays, but Aunt Pam had saved me some, and there was pork and baked potatoes in the oven, fresh tomatoes and cucumbers on the counter. The oven stuff was a little dry, but I was not a picky boy in those days, as long as you didn't try to make me eat oysters.

I could not believe that a day of playing ball in the sun would make a person even more tired than a day of thinning apples, but I felt every molecule of my body as I climbed the slope to my cabin, flashlight in one hand and a copy of the August issue of *Sport* in the other. It had Yogi Berra on the cover and a story about Ned Garver living the last place life inside. I will never forget the story of Ned Garver asking for a raise.

"I won twenty games for a last place team."

"Oh yeah? Where would we have finished if you'd just won ten?"

When I was twenty and visiting Oliver during a leave from the air force base in Manitoba, I wore dark glasses all the time, hung a cigarette off my bottom lip, slouched in chairs and mumbled, until Wendy proffered the opinion that I was not James Dean, before she went on to use the word "mature" that I had been hearing so much of over the years.

Oh, it seems as if I spent the entire second half of my pre-adult life mooning over Wendy Love or trying to impress her with my uniqueness. But it was not Wendy Love that I dreamed of that night in my picker's cabin among the trees. According to the short diary note that I scratched out in code the next day, I passed every second of my sleeping time in the intimate company of the red-headed art teacher.

I wish I could remember her name. In my dream, which I must have commenced a few minutes after I put away Ned Garver and extinguished the lantern, she was dressed as she always was at the bowling alley. She had that white loose jersey kind of top and a swishy black and white and red checked skirt. I had quite often seen her passing our house on her way from school to downtown, walking in one of those dresses that gave a boy a pretty good idea about the dimensions of her chest and bum. But I was mainly attracted to her legs.

In my dream I was licking those legs. Once in a while she would move one to give me a new angle. She was sitting on a corner of her home room desk, and there was no one else anywhere in the school, unless the janitor was banging around the furnace room looking for trouble. She had all her clothes on, a summer dress and high-heeled shoes, but no stockings. Her skirt was hiked up to her waist, and I was licking her legs. Ankles, feet, calves, especially calves, and when she lay back on the wide desk I licked her thighs.

Whenever I read the word "thigh" in a book, as long as it was attached to a woman or a girl, I got a buzz. Now in my dream, and I don't remember whether I thought it was not a dream in my dream, she moved one thigh farther away from the other thigh, and I shoved my face in. I don't remember whether it was warm, only that these were muscular thighs. They were longer than Miss Verge's.

"Stop it," said the teacher with the red hair, but she had both hands on my head, so I couldn't have moved if I had wanted to. I kissed her smooth skin and licked where I had kissed. There was no way I could have learned this anywhere, but I was giving myself to the art teacher.

This was a dream, but I was still surprised to notice that all my clothes had come off. I took one of her high-heeled shoes in my hand and started to remove it.

"Leave it on," she said. And then since this was a dream anyway, all the rest of her clothes were off and we were no longer in the classroom but in the grandstand of the ballpark in Oliver. We were sitting side by side in a row near the bottom. I had an erection, not all that unusual that year.

"Oh, this is what you want," said the art teacher, and reaching over with her far hand, she wrapped her fingers around my little pole.

Then it was all over — I was awake in my orchard home, and it was all over my midsection and upper legs and the sheet.

IT WAS NOT the first time I had ejaculated for the image of our art teacher, and I was not the only youth in the south Okanagan who thought about her while seeking lonesome pleasures. But it was the first time she had appeared in my dreams. Even Miss

Verge had never been in my dreams. Wendy had, but that was to be expected.

The funny thing is that I don't remember whether Polly and Winnie ever showed up in my sleep. I had the vague hots for Polly and more specific hots for Winnie.

Once apricot season was over and the really hot air of August lay on the orchard rows, Uncle Gerry had to hire a lot of peach and pear pickers. The Aikins ranch had more peach acreage than most orchards, and once those things got big and coloured, you needed a crew that could move. If you were picking cherries or apples or prunes you just stripped the trees of fruit, but if you were after peaches or pears, you had to pick to size and colour. Every tree had to be picked three or four or sometimes even five times.

Nowadays young French Canadians supply a lot of the casual work in the orchards of the south Okanagan on the BC side, while Mexicans do it on the Washington side. But back then in the fifties, there were a lot of Doukhobor workers in our orchards. At first I thought that Polly and Winnie were sisters, but it turned out that Winnie was Polly's mother. I think Polly was probably about sixteen years old, but it was hard to say. We anglo boys always thought those Russian girls got sexy really young. So a thirteen-year-old Doukhobor girl would be way sexier than a seventeen-year-old WASP girl. And if Polly was, say, fifteen, Winnie might have been in her early thirties. She was a lot sexier than any women I knew who were in their early thirties.

My mother was in her early thirties, but she wasn't sexy, not as far as I could see, anyway. Mrs. Wilkins next door was pretty sexy, if you were just keeping track of tits or at least brassieres.

But it was hard to figure out whether Polly and Winnie were wearing brassieres. Maybe Doukhobor women wore home-made clothing, including plain cloth brassieres with no elastic. Anyway, Polly and Winnie both wore faded cotton skirts and men's shirts with the sleeves rolled up. They had sweat under their arms and down their backbones, and sometimes the cloth adhered to their nice big bums.

You do know that we bumpkins believed that these people were not regular Christians, and they were not descended from any Brits or Western Europeans, and they had strange semi-Oriental religious beliefs that might have included nakedness. We hoped that their religion and social strictures did not have anything to prevent screwing guys in the long grass, or showing teenaged boys stuff they had never dreamed of. The only thing we did not agree on was whether it would be best to plank a teenaged one or an older one.

Polly had long blonde hair that hung straight but got sweaty and plastered on her face and neck. Sweat ran down her face and once in a while you would see her lick it off her upper lip, and for some reason this would make you get a semi-hard on. Winnie was experienced. She had a daughter, so she must have known more stuff than her daughter did, and had had time to perfect whatever it was she knew. I watched her reach up and grab both sides of a sixteen-foot picking ladder to move it around her tree, and I looked down the rolled sleeve of her shirt, and I saw it, I was sure I had seen it. How I wished that the world would forget all its rules and I could reach and hold it, just for a minute.

This sort of thing was beginning to occupy my attention and desire more than the Max Brand Silvertip novels I was reading. Part of me took that as a bad sign. Another part considered it to be a feature of growing up. I did not, however, submit it to Wendy as evidence of my approaching maturity.

Of course there were all kinds of ill-informed rumours about the generous sexual practices of Doukhobor girls, and Winnie and Polly did not avert those. The part of me that believed in a world pictured by the New Testament and *World's Finest Comics* and *Silvertip's Strike* said that these rumours were the wishful fictionalizing of dirty young minds. The part of me that owed its life to biochemicals looked at the sweat holding Polly's shirt to her torso and longed for the nerve to talk to her alone.

In the tourist advertisements in magazine and newspapers, peaches were picked by conventionally attractive young women wearing halter tops and white shorts. Try that for a day, ladies, and you will come back with sunburn and scratches and insect bites and peach fuzz in all your sweaty creases. In real life women wore hats and long-sleeved shirts and their husband's or father's long pants and boots of some sort. Polly and Winnie were the first females I had ever seen picking in long skirts. Well, long enough to cover everything above their ankles, except when they twirled for some reason, or a breeze came up.

I emptied my peaches into a crate and begged for a medium to high wind. I thought about walking under Polly's ladder to see what kind of luck I would have. I fantasized declaring my love for her, ripping my shirt open to show her my heart. I wanted to share a peach fuzz itch with her, even imagined standing naked, back to back with her. I wanted to put on a blindfold and walk into her cabin after dark. I often cast a furtive glance, hoping to spy a nipple bulge against her shirt front.

On Sunday Polly came to our home game without her mother. I did not dare hope that she was there to watch me, and then I hoped she hadn't, because I went 0 for 4 with a walk. Luckily I did not commit an error at second, even though I took my eye off the ball often, to look at her sitting at the top of our four-step bleacher in her Sunday outfit, a girl's short-sleeved shirt and a clean skirt that came down to her calves. I made up my mind, after eight innings of interior debate, to talk to her after the game, but when it was over and I looked at the bleacher she was not there. I looked in all directions. She had disappeared.

That night I thought about her in her Sunday outfit.

What about my true heart for Wendy Love? Come on, I was under sixteen years old, an innocent boy with an erection. I was truly and eternally in love with Wendy, but look at it this way — what if I *did* happen to get lucky with Polly, or better yet, with her mother? Wouldn't I then come to Wendy with both an experience and a comparison in which she would shine?

All right, then. I didn't have to enjoy Polly's favours entirely. What if I just got to feel her, feel those breasts I could almost see or at least imagine that I could almost see, feel her back and her bum and her legs? What if I was just able to kiss the area between her neck and her bosom? When I got a particularly large peach in the palm of my hand I stopped for a while. When you pick peaches you get paid by the hour to discourage loading your crates with immature fruit.

I heard Polly and Winnie talking to each other in Russian, and I was off on a lifetime of getting crushes on women speaking European languages. Were they talking about me, ever? Did they make fun of the virgin boy with the pimples? But wait. What about Miss Verge? Hadn't she relieved me of my virginity? Okay, I was an innocent. Was I engaged in this sophistry then, or now?

Now that I remember, in my cartooning I had learned how to draw faces in profile and women's breasts in one-quarter profile. I drew them the way Al Capp did. They were always voluptuous, not at all like Wendy's nice little mounds. Sunny side up, I called them when she couldn't hear. I never made the kinds of crude sexual drawings one might sometimes find in the washrooms at school or the Scout Hall.

"Hi," I said to Polly and Winnie one morning, and then every morning after that.

"Hi," said Winnie. Her daughter never said anything. Was that a hopeful sign?

But I could not get any further with words. I was too shy, as usual but even more so, baffled by lust and curiosity. They must have felt that they were in a place where they were surrounded by people from another story, and I'll bet that they had good reason to believe that they were surrounded by lust and curiosity.

I would always have trouble with words in any social situation. I did not know how to talk to people easily, how to let things be imperfect and find their own way. So with Wendy I could talk like mad as long as I was acting or bragging or pretending, or if we were constructing one of our fantasies — our future children and their names, for example. With Miss Verge I didn't have to say anything. I did not have to approach. I was afraid to ask. As for Jeanette, the situation was perhaps like the one with Polly and Winnie — Jeanette was from a somewhat different world, one holding secrets and customs that might seem mysterious or dangerous to a biscuit boy like me. But I did not, it seemed to me, lust for her. I wanted to discover her and protect her. Still, at least once a night I remembered what I saw when she held her shirt open for two seconds.

ᕙ⎯ᕗ

I KNEW WHERE Polly and Winnie's cabin was, and I knew that there was a rule that no one was allowed to go near it. Was it an orchard rule? Did my uncle Gerry make it up? Did Mr. Aikins make it up years and years ago? I think it was Paddy who told me about it, and not directly. There are a lot of horny guys in any orchard. Still, while I played cards with my uncle and aunt in their warm kitchen, I thought about creeping from tree to tree. I would often take a few unnecessary steps in their direction, but I knew that I was the kind of kid who would never grab the brass ring. In fact in all the merry-go-rounds I had seen, there had been no brass rings. I took it to be one of those things the American kids got, like the stuff they could send Popsicle® bags away for. I would never get my picture on the cover of a magazine. I would never get to see a fight at Madison Square Garden. I would never have my own pair of baseball spikes, even.

So, no, I would never hear a light tap at my cabin door and open it to see Polly there, or Winnie, or — oh lord — both of them. How would we three fit in my cot? What would we do? It was hard to imagine all the things we might do when I didn't really know what people did, except feel and put it in and all that. But to have them both there and naked and maybe sweating and murmuring in Russian. That did the trick, and a little later I was off to sleep. But if only they could see how ashamed I would be.

CHAPTER 15

*M*Y FAVOURITE JOB around the orchard was driving the tractor. I did not have a driver's licence, being too young and all, but a year before I had guest-driven a small Ford tractor at an orchard where Nigel Lamb was playing more than working. I have to take us back now to the early summer, before the Bing cherries were dark enough and big enough for picking, and most of the work was early apple thinning and hauling prop poles from their teepees to various stations on the ranch. I had forgotten those prop teepees till just now. How else would you store lodgepole pine trunks with the branches chopped off? I liked those conical structures, and so did field mice and chipmunks, who would scatter when you pulled down the props and laid them longwise on the wagon.

Boys driving tractors are really adolescents acquiring a high regard for their own sexual likelihood. I faintly sensed that when I sat up on the seat of that little grey Ford tractor, with the compression snout out front of my crotch. It is part of nature's plan that teenaged lads should roar around fruit groves on loud motorized phalluses, covered with sweat and striped with grime.

Now in midsummer, with the work eased back from emer-
gency schedules, my father had arrived to spend the night at the
house, then to leave with Uncle Gerry for a three-day hunting
trip somewhere up in the mountains. Normally hunting season,
at least for deer, was in October, but there must have been a special cull that year, so the brothers were off in their boots and red
vests, and Paddy was left in charge of the small crew of which I
was the youngest member by far.

Driving a tractor is not all that difficult, as long as you are
going straight ahead on level ground, with no trailer. But orchard
tractors are not meant for driving with no trailer, and on the
Aikins ranch there was precious little level ground, perched as
we were on the edge of a cliff above the lake, and where there are
hundreds and thousands of fruit trees in an orchard, you have to
turn eventually, turn with a trailer load of props or boxes. And
a lot of the time you have to travel in reverse, and when this
involves a loaded trailer, you practically need a degree in physics to figure out what direction to turn the steering wheel — if
you have a tractor with a steering wheel.

The first tractor Paddy plunked me on was a relic of an earlier
age in another jurisdiction. It was a lot bigger than most, and its
brand name was Oliver. In my home town with that same name
I had never seen one. There was only one wheel in the front, and
the two back wheels were enormous, so that when I sat on the
high metal saddle between them I felt that I might be perilous to
all plant life.

I wasted a lot of time turning the wheel the wrong way when
I backed up, sometimes jackknifing too close to some tender tree
with baby apples on it. A few times I had to unhook the trailer
and back the Oliver up to it from another angle. My happiest
time was spent tooling along the dusty orchard road toward the
warehouse or the props teepee. Often I had to drive through a

patch of sprinkler-moistened dirt, and I loved the marks made by the deep tread on those wheels. Once, when no one was looking, I nearly lost us all, trailer, props, Oliver and teenage sportswriter, over the lip of the cliff. If we had slid backward a few more feet, and if I had survived the fall, I would not have climbed the hill to collect my pay cheque. I would have lit out for Ecuador.

Ah, high bright tractor wheels!

When I put a hole in one of those big tires, I didn't think of Ecuador, but the idea of, say, California came to mind. I may as well mention that all my life, at school, in the air force, in my relationships, it has been explained to me that I am a fuckup. I came to believe it early. And all my life I've tried to find a way to live with the fact. As sure as God made little green apples and I learned to thin them, I was an orchard fuckup.

I don't know how I got a hole in the Oliver's tire. The tractor had been around so long that hardly anyone knew there was such a thing, a huge three-wheel machine with a strange name, and no one had ever put it out of commission before. I found out that those big heavy tires were full of water! They were as heavy as a couple of swimming pools. Now I had become the only Okanagan boy ever to let the water out of one while his father and his ramrod were away on a hunting trip. I could see a month's paycheque flying back where it came from.

Paddy looked at the slowly emptying tire, took out his jack-knife, cleaned out his pipe bowl, and stayed calm. I stood there for a while, thinking about how every minute was a cent I was supposed to be earning. Paddy thumbed some new tobacco into his pipe and put his pouch back into a pocket inside his vest.

"I'm going to have to teach you how to drive Old Snuffy," he said.

He was talking about the other tractor, the one that looked like the first bulldozer ever made. It had lugs like a tank's instead of wheels, noisy hand levers instead of a steering wheel, and a high metal seat with no padding.

"Thing'll shake every drop of piss outa your kidneys," said Paddy.

Nobody knew what brand of machine it was. It could have been an early Caterpillar, but there weren't any words on it anywhere. Maybe there never were. Maybe it was just put together by some oilrag genius out of parts found by the side of the road. Old Snuffy had an exhaust pipe that went straight up, and the first piece of advice Paddy gave me was not to touch that pipe, even with my work gloves on.

"Damned thing's hotter than my drainpipe was forty years ago," he said.

So I got up on that sucker and tried to learn the controls. There was no gas pedal, just a lever you pushed forward and back. There was a brake lever for each set of lugs. If you pulled the right one you got a sudden right turn as that lug stopped dead and the other dug up dirt alongside you. You had to stop thinking in circles and start thinking in straight lines. I'll never get this right, I thought. I'm probably too much of a fuckup. I'll take out a line of peach trees.

Once you started it up and pushed on the lever for power, you couldn't get any more advice from Paddy. Old Snuffy was so loud you could hear him from anywhere on the ranch. I'd never be able to knock off in some far corner and sit back to Tom Sawyer the sky.

It took a long time to learn how to back up with a trailer load of full boxes with that thing, because not only did you have to remember to turn left to go right, but you had to learn how to do it with levers instead of a wheel, and all this while looking over your shoulder behind you. I told myself to be more circumspect, a word I had learned only the other night, when approaching the cliffs.

But boy, was it fun roaring along the dusty orchard road with that big old bulldozer thing in front of my bouncing steel saddle. It was so goddamned loud, and I was covered in dust and sweat, far beyond itchy, ready to run over anything that tried to get in my way. I sang at the top of my lungs beside the rattling exhaust pipe, not hearing the words at all. My kidneys were jiggling. I must have looked like a modern shaggy hero.

⁓

I HONESTLY CAN'T remember what Uncle Gerry said when they got back from hunting. Both he and my father had unshaven faces, looked like a couple of backcountry rifle rubes, should have had a jug of corn licker.

I think that Uncle Gerry became the tractor guy, and I remember that he went at it with no dreams of glamour and valour and all that ace pilot business, but as a serious job, eyes on the ground in front of him as he flang those gears around. It was back to my ladder and boots for me.

Speaking of which, I should have mentioned long ago that they were not properly my boots, but a pair nearly my size that had been left behind by some itinerant picker the year before. After the third week I remembered to buy a pair of boot laces in Penticton, and they were a significant improvement over the multisourced strings that I had inherited. It was terrific to have laces long enough for the boots and all one piece each instead of black lace knotted to butcher string, and so on.

But the nail in the heel was another story. I can't right now tell you which heel the nail was in but I can tell you that I tried just about every remedy a boy could think of during that hot summer. I was pretty well used to nails in shoes. But going to school with a nail in your foot is different from working ten hours a day with one. Sometimes you could get a hammer and whang them inside the shoe, but boots are awkward for whanging. You could get a screwdriver or chisel and put the business end on the nail and whang the handle of the chisel or screwdriver, but you usually just did a lot of damage to the nail. The one I am talking about I managed to bend, so that I had a blunt nail arch digging into my heel, which is a lot better than a nail point. But your sock would get a hole, eh? And then a bigger hole. And your foot would get a sore and it wouldn't get time to crust over, and there was a lot of blood in your socks. What a nuisance. And all that limping.

So eventually you mainly resorted to packing things inside the heel of your boot and over the nail. A folded up Sportsman cigarettes package. A spare sock that had already suffered too much damage. Fold after fold of toilet paper, swiped from Auntie Pam's indoor toilet. A leather tongue off an even worse boot. That was the best, but every half hour you had to take your boot off and put the tongue back over the bent nail. Okay, a sore heel was part of the working life. So I would have a limp for the first half of the school year. It would make me romantic, and garner me the sympathy of sweet girls, a sympathy that I could fashion into something more exciting. I took my boots off as soon as the work day was over.

I practised limping for Polly and Winnie. All I got was a mock limp from Polly, who did not look romantic at all. So I tried walking without a limp. That in itself should have looked valorous, but it did not succeed any better. Polly and Winnie just did not flirt. They did not need to. Just to watch the way Polly's gingham dress fluttered around her bare legs when she was sticking her ladder up in a new spot was enough to make me stop thinking about the Dodgers outfield — Furillo, Snider, and was it Pafko?

Whenever he caught me staring, Paddy would clear his throat, pretending that he had got a tobacco dribble in his mouth or something. He kept his pipe in his mouth every minute of the day except for the two minutes it took him to consume his sandwich at lunch. I was just beginning to smoke cigarettes, Sportsman, saving the yellow packages with the fishing flies on the back, but I never smoked while I was picking. When I drove one of the tractors I would hold a cigarette in the corner of my mouth, like a new Humphrey Bogart, and I had scars on my left shoulder from turning to check my trailer and sticking burning Sportsmans against my bare skin.

I sometimes wonder whether Paddy ever saw me staring at the Doukhobor cabin window from the apple tree darkness. If so, he didn't clear his throat after the sun went down. Winnie and Polly had a cabin no bigger than mine, but they had a wider cot. From my vantage place on the lowest branch of a Winesap, I could catch a glimpse of it through the slight gap between edge of window and edge of curtain. Once I just about fell out of my tree when the door suddenly opened and Polly stepped down the two wooden steps and hiked without a flashlight toward the outhouse. As the door swung shut I saw Winnie. She was leaning over a basin of water and placing a washcloth on her face. She was wearing some kind of cotton nightgown, I guess. Her breasts were hanging nicely but I could not really see them. I only knew they were there. I was a pinsetter boy up a tree.

The next night in my cabin I stood naked and turned around some before I got into my bed to start reading. Just in case Polly or Winnie or both were up a tree out there. Or Aunt Pam. That was a thought that came to me suddenly. A shiver of fear went up and down my body as my innocent cock rose, and now I was really a bit scared so I jumped into bed and picked up my new copy of *Baseball* magazine. The cover was black and white and red all over. I read a little, but not much.

⌐⟶

I JUST HAVE the vaguest images of Polly's face left in my memory bank, and even less of her mother's. What I do have might be invented from whole cloth, or from the images I do have of the cloth that covered just about their whole bodies but in such a way that you might prefer that to nakedness. I see long light brown hair blown in the breeze around their faces or moist with sweat and lying across their cheeks. So their long thin dresses, wind or sweat. I see that roundish Russian beauty you can't help associating with potatoes and warm beds and tractor mud. While I was entranced by Moonbeam McSwine, she was no Russian and I never saw her legs move up a ladder.

When you are a fifteen-year-old boy, or at least when I was a fifteen-year-old boy, even the women in the newspaper comics or comic books could turn you on in a second. I was a mountain-climbing kid, and there were times when I onanized on the pine needles on the forest floor, except that we did not really have a forest — it was more like a tree, then some dry couch grass, then another tree, then some rocks, then another tree.

As to the women in the comics, there were some good ones in *Terry and the Pirates*, though I can't remember their names. The Dragon Lady was kind of scary, and showed up transmogrified to an empress in one of my recurrent dreams. I'd be on a sloping tile floor, sweating in my torn clothing, trying to crawl uphill toward this magisterial and cruel figure who was probably going to have me whipped if I reached her feet anyway.

Al Capp was the best, though. Daisy Mae was pretty well as pulchritudinous as Moonbeam McSwine, even though she was blond and did not hang out in the pigsty mud. Stupefyin' Jones had me a little scared. Betty and Veronica didn't raise much more of a buzz than did Miz Beasley. Wonder Woman was an interesting prospect, and though I did not know why, I approved of her high red boots and golden lasso. And Sheena of the Jungle? Those torn shorts, and all those vines! I pictured her in my orchard.

⌒〜⌐

ALL THIS TIME my father was taking care of the scorekeeping in Oliver, and writing the weekly stories for the Penticton *Herald* and the Oliver *Chronicle*. Today, five and a half decades later, my mother reads the *Herald* in her Oliver sitting room, and here in Vancouver I get the *Chronicle* in the mail every Friday. I scan the stories of high school graduations and automobile accidents for family names. I look at the obits every week and check to see how many of the people I knew and how many of them were older than I.

The *Chronicle* now has a weekly photo item called, unfortunately, "Turning Back the Clock on Time." Last week it featured a group photograph of all the Girl Guides of 1948, the greatest year in the history of human civilization. This means that it included modestly uniformed girls about my age at the time, some a year ahead of me, others in my grade, the rest a year behind me. They were all about thirteen or fourteen, let's say. Here I am, an old gink, but I recognized all their faces, and recalled nearly all their names. A few of them are dead. All the rest are old ladies now. Many of them I saw at a fiftieth high school grad reunion a couple of years ago.

You cannot turn back the clock, on time or on anything else. But I know all those girls. I acted in plays with some of them. I kissed a very few. I never had sex with any of them. You'd need a different kind of group photograph for that.

Barbara Gregory, my first girlfriend, is in that picture. Sylvia MacIntosh, with whom I was in love in grade nine and grade ten, is in it. And Wendy Love is in it, right in the centre, turned into a bone face by the camera's crude flash, her hair back tight, her lips almost nonexistent. In fact, just about every girl in junior high was in the Girl Guides. That's the way things were back then up there in that valley. But Jeanette MacArthur is not in that photograph.

I think I know why. Jeanette didn't have anyone in her family who could or would shell out the money it would take to acquire or fabricate a Girl Guide outfit and pay whatever dues there were and so forth. I know that she was probably embarrassed about it. Maybe she was the only girl in grade eight not to be in Girl Guides. Or maybe she was forbidden to join such a group because of her religion. No, I don't remember anything about her religion, and if she were in some oddball religion, all the kids would have known about it and talked about it. I don't think the Doukhobor kids over in the next valley were allowed to join the Girl Guides, because they might appear to be somehow military in those outfits. I'm betting that Polly was never a Girl Guide.

Those Girl Guide uniforms used a lot of heavy blue cloth. They were not in any way erotic, not obviously. They were buttoned up right to the collar, and they fell in pleats or some kind of folds to below the knees. The sleeves were long and the berets were not at all saucy. You had to work your imagination hard to picture bare legs above long stockings under dark blue pleats. It was an effort to picture bare thighs moving apart in the darkness inside those grandmotherly dresses. To let your fancy find a reason to hesitate at loose panties up there in the heat.

I was working in an orchard, with sexual pictures rolling through my head, not a sign of a whisker on my chin. I possessed, that summer, a bifurcated mind. Part of my intracranial movie theatre showed the pictures you would expect a male virgin would project. Yet the same cinema house offered footage of real life adventures with Miss Verge. I was the opposite of the boy that bragged of sexual conquests he had never made — I kept quiet about achieving what was usually encountered only in fantasy at that age at that time. Not the mate or instructress one might choose for one's own fantasy, but strange dynamite in a beautiful country pond.

But where was Jeanette MacArthur the day that this picture was taken? Was she in her house, mopping the kitchen's linoleum floor? The picture was taken two or three years before I had squatted in the tulies and spied on the back of Jeanette's house.

I try to imagine Jeanette in a Girl Guide uniform, and I can do it, but everything is wrong. She did not tie the neckerchief correctly. Her shoes are the wrong colour. There is a string hanging from the hem, and the hem is too high. The beret is shoved up in the front. She has a scowl on her face that could have neutralized the fixer in the photographer's darkroom tray.

I don't try to imagine Jeanette bare naked now, but I did back there in that orchard over the clay cliffs on the east side of Lake Okanagan. The image kept trying to slide away, like raw calf's liver off a plate. See what happens when I try to use a simile? Like mercury on a desk top. Like a ground ball off your glove in late innings. Like those little black blobs in the middle of your eyesight. Like a simile in the hands of a memoirist trying to keep his unconscious mind from taking over the balcony in an earthquake.

I would try to see her naked and her clothes, worn out as they were, would reappear on her body. I had seen her bare breasts for two seconds. Distant tree fruit, they were. I thought of them while I was removing a peach from a branch. Once in a while I would kiss a peach. I wonder whether Paddy ever did that. When Polly came down her ladder with the intent of repositioning it her breasts moved around inside her thin dress in such a way as to make my throat go dry. But doing the same thing, Jeanette would be a solid such as we learned about in grade ten science. She was not an awkward girl — it was just that she had not learned or given in to the notion that teenaged girls were syrup and ponies. She was more like a patio wall. (See, you start on similes, and that is what happens).

Still, I was worried about her. I knew that all the other guys in my class could ignore her without worrying about it. I guess I cared about her. I was not, as my vocabulary put it then, "madly, passionately, hopelessly" in love with her. I thought that down there in her unpainted house on Sawmill Road something was happening to her on a regular basis. It might have just been the deprivation of hope. It might have been something unspeakable because it was not known about. She never crossed the irrigation ditch bridge with a smile on her face. She did not play a clarinet in the school band. She did not wander around the community hall grounds during the track meet.

Up my tree, I tried to imagine Wendy with her clothes off, that body that was unlike the drawings of Al Capp, in that her waist did not go way in and her hips did not go way out. The line down her side was nearly straight. During the coming Fall I would run my hand down from her armpit to her ankle, and I would like it just fine, though my heart would be trying to pound its way out. But here in late August, peach fuzz on my sweaty neck, I tried to imagine a naked Wendy Love and kept getting a nearly naked Polly Horkoff.

And when the month came to an end, and the first weekend of September flipped by, I had not once touched daughter or mother, much less aunt. I had touched myself a number of times, Onan among the tree trunks, a part-time ballplayer near a cliff, approaching manhood with a farmer's tan and an innocent imagination.

When it came time to go back to school in Oliver, I was a returning hero in my mind, a new smoking habit and long sweaty hair to prove it. My mother sat me down in her kitchen and took care of the hair. But I had to go south of town to the Home gas station store to buy the Sportsman's.

CHAPTER *16*

I NEVER BOUGHT into the myth that you were supposed to dis-
like school. I liked it a lot. For one thing, school did not entail
getting up too early and putting on boots and heading out to the
orchard or down to the packing house. You might have to hold
down a job as a student, but it could take only about an hour or
two a day of your time. At school I got to show off my skills as
a wiseacre, and sometimes as a stage actor. I got to play in the
band and sing in the choir. I kept the scorebook at the basketball
games. For a while Will and I had a sort of radio show on the
school PA system, a half-hour of every lunch break. We scripted
and performed skits and played my 45 rpm records of Frankie
Laine and Louis Armstrong. I wasn't trying to get popular — I
knew that would never happen. I did not belong to the photog-
raphy club because Will and I had our own darkroom. I did not
write for the *Scroll*, the student newspaper, because I was writing
for the Penticton *Herald* and Oliver *Chronicle*.

So the start of a new school year was always interesting. I
might even have a new pair of corduroy pants. We were into
what we called "drapes" then, what the eastern newspapers

called "pegged pants," and the Vancouver teenagers called "strides," trousers that were maybe ten inches around the ankle and forty inches at the knees. The best ones were the "Chinks" from Vancouver. These were made of black denim, and had six inches of white buttons above the belt.

That September, Southern Okanagan High School smelled good. I sniffed and sniffed all day the first week. The fresh wax on the hall floor, the polish on any wood that happened to be employed by the modernist postwar architects, the invisible cleanser on the sparkling windows, the glue and chalk and vinyl, made my glossy head swim. You could smell the new clothes on the girls, the shine on their shoes and the perfume in their handkerchiefs. Within the first hour I had ink stains on my shirt and arms, but the odours wafting from room to room and down the hall spoke to me of freshness, of a chance to start again and get it right this time.

Actually, I think that last part is bullshit.

But it was exciting. The gymnasium and the changing rooms still smelled like cleanser and wax rather than gooey feet and rancid armpits.

I sniffed Wendy even though she did not have any new clothes. I was discreet — I placed my head near her shoulder and breathed in the familiar Wendyness of her hair.

"I wish you were Pooh instead of Tigger," she said.

What was she talking about? She wanted me to be a piece of shit? Then I remembered, but I decided to string her along.

"What instead of who?"

She just looked at me for a count of, I don't know, maybe twenty-four. I took the opportunity to admire her one crooked front tooth.

"Winnie-the-Pooh," she said at last. "Surely you recall that I assumed responsibility for your education in matters literary last Spring?"

When she said something like that, her English accent came back, which was part of the reason I loved her. Her looks made her a little vulnerable, what with her small breasts and thick ankles and lack of eyebrows, but her English accent gave her a kind of authority. I would do whatever I could to provoke Wendy's English accent.

"I have read *Fiddlefoot*," I said, "but not your Pooh."

"What foot?" she enquired, her scanty eyebrows rising, the "what" sounding a lot like "wote" to my OK Valley ear.

"*Fiddlefoot*, by Luke Short. It's about a chicken-hearted drifter who takes a stand, and a lot of people get shot."

"You will be disappointed in Pooh. No one gets shot. It is the product of a civilized country."

"Well, then, so are you," I said, and I placed my fingers in the small of her back. It was about the only trick I knew.

"I would think more of you if you had read *Winnie-the-Pooh*."

"I will permit you to read it to me. With an English accent."

"I have done so. I cannot imagine that you do not recall. You who can remember a baseball player's bashing average."

"I was too busy admiring your lovely foreign accent. Read it to me once more."

And so she did. She was clearly onto me, I knew, but she played along for her own purposes. Some of the most memorable experiences I would ever have would be those Sunday afternoons listening to my fiancée read chapters from *The House on Pooh Corner*. I was well-behaved because I felt the importance of those hours. I never felt Wendy up while she was doing the voices of Pooh and Eeyore and Tigger while I lay on the floor of her verandah and later that fall in her living room.

I wished that she would feel me up, but then again I didn't. I had embarrassment and shyness wrapped around my desire. So I made do with feeling myself up and imagining her. All the while wondering about that. So I listened to the adventures of Pooh, and I really was glad that she was reading the stories with an English accent, and even more glad that she adjusted her voice when it came time for dialogue between Pooh and his friends. At first these stories had seemed foreign to me, but after a few weeks I had a sort of feeling that I was an English boy who had fetched up in the Okanagan Valley by chance. I felt as if the stories that Wendy was reading to me were coming out of my own proper home. I would not tell this to anyone. But fifteen years later, when I was at the pointy end of a ferry boat approaching the white cliffs of Dover I felt as if I were coming home or something. Enough about that. Now I knew why she called me Tigger, and she would not be the last female human to do that.

⌐⌐ↄ

I GUESS THAT this is the place and time to describe a scene I have been thinking of for the past hundred pages.

The previous winter my mother had somehow put the down payment on a little house on the southwest edge of Tuc-el-Nuit Lake, the last property before the beach that made up the main swimming place in Oliver in those days. It was not much more than a shack, a brown thing with shingles under pine boughs and surrounded by runaway bushes and vines. There were bulrushes in front of it, and reeds in the water. I don't think anyone had lived in it legally for a few years. It had probably been owned by a beer-drinking old widower with tobacco stains on his grey moustache, one of those Oliver coots with holes in his hat. He was a lucky man when my mother came around with an offer.

From then on, when we could spare time from school and people's orchards and other jobs, my parents and I would be over at the place pulling weeds or wheelbarrowing rocks or gathering up the fallen fence. The fenceposts were smooth grey wood with insect holes, the wire rusty from having lain under snow for several winters. I found the skeleton of a cat under the boards that acted as a front step. There was a wasp's nest the size of a beach ball in the attic. Pieces of broken brown glass could be found a foot down in what had once been an attempt at a vegetable garden on the slope up to the Tuc-el-Nuit Lake road, which was still made of dirt in those days.

One Sunday in the middle of the summer, when I was home for the weekend from Naramata, my dad and I were out at the place pulling weeds and chopping brush. My dad was wearing work gloves, but there were some three-leaved weeds he would not touch.

"That's poison ivy," he said. "Don't touch it with your bare hands."

Of course I knew it was poison ivy. I was familiar with all the poison things here in the south Okanagan. We had rattlesnakes in the hills and sometimes our back yards. We had black widow spiders in the cellar. I had seen one scorpion in front of my face while climbing the shale above Gallagher Lake. But I figured I was immune to poison ivy. I had been yanking it out barehanded all summer. We always told each other that a person's immunities changed every seven years. Things were always changing every seven years. John Jalovec said that every seven years your whole body has replaced every cell. I hoped I still had a few years left of being immune to poison ivy.

My father was the opposite. If he touched poison ivy his skin would be covered with sores and rashes and his eyes would be swollen shut. If he walked on poison ivy leaves and touched his shoes at the end of the day, he could look forward to rashes and swellings two days later. It would even happen if he touched the hoe I had been chopping it with. If he got near my dog Dinky and Dinky had brushed a poison ivy leaf yesterday, off he'd go.

If I threw poison ivy on our weed fire and the smoke went in his direction, he'd be covered with blisters in two days. You should have seen my dad resisting the compulsion to scratch his itches — he was heroic.

Wasps were an even worse threat to my dad. Wasps and bees and hornets and yellowjackets could kill him if a bunch hit him at once. One wasp bite and he would be in bed with a fever, sweating and eyes swollen shut. Not me. I used to get stung by those things, and I didn't like it, but all I got was pain followed by itch. Once at the spillway I stepped on a wasp and got stung on the sole of my foot. It hurt like the dickens and was hard to scratch. I figured I must be near the bad part of my seven-year wasp susceptibility.

A few years later, when I was going with Joan and listening to a lot of classical music, I fell in love with the music of Alban Berg. I heard that he had died after stepping on a wasp. There he was, banned from the auditorium by Hitler, and he steps on a wasp. He died twenty-three days after I was born. While he was alive he was crazy about the number 23. He would begin and finish composing a work on the 23rd day of the month. Then he died in his prime. I wonder whether my father ever heard *Wozzek*.

I wonder whether Wendy ever played any Berg on her family's piano. I doubt it. I do remember asking her to play some of Grieg's lyric pieces, and she seemed to think that they were pretty modern. I wish I could go back now and ask her how she felt about Berg and Picasso and Ezra Pound, but I think I know.

Nowadays when I visit Oliver I drive from place to place, but back then we just naturally walked, once we had outgrown our bikes. One Saturday in early October, when the orchardists figured they could get the remainder of their apples in without any schoolkid help, Wendy and I held hands and walked out to the lake. I don't know how far it was. Not as far as the walk to Will's place on the other side of the water. Probably about a mile and a half. When I was twelve and had my paper route I used to walk or ride my bike right by the dark shack that would one day be my mother's property. In those days it had been almost hidden by piles of tumbleweeds.

I told my mother that we were going to do a little weed pulling, so she gave me the key and reminded me that the work gloves were inside the back door. My dad was in Penticton, at some teachers' meeting. Otherwise he would have driven us to the lake and stayed around for an afternoon of cleaning up. Wendy and I held hands, as we always did, and I sang to her, like a musical comedy star. She pretended that I was not missing the notes, and I had little idea that I was less perfect than Gene Kelly.

> *I look at you and suddenly*
> *Something in your eyes I see*
> *Soon begins bewitching me*

We actually, as I recall, were going to do some weeding. But first I had to show Wendy around the house, what there was of it. There was a kitchen and two little bedrooms and a tiny bathroom and a small living room with a couch and a trilight in it. That didn't take long. I showed her around the outside, showed her where my dad and I had destroyed a lot of vegetative snarl and built a bending pathway to the edge of the water. There was no real beach yet, just a gradual change from cat tails growing out of the soil and reeds sticking up out of the water. There was a bit of a smell — I don't know whether the place had a leaking septic tank or no septic tank at all.

We were holding hands as much as we could, even while squeezing through the narrow doors and negotiating right-angle turns more quickly than you would do in an average house. This place made Wendy's parents' place seem large and well-appointed.

So naturally, as I was used to doing in those days, I eventually folded her in my arms and kissed her lips. Narrow as they were, they were a great pleasure to kiss, and I have to admit that she had taught me how to kiss a girlfriend as if she were not a granny.

"I cannot bear the harsh sunlight in here," I said, and proceeded to pull down the blinds at the living room windows.

It would have been smoother if I had just done that stage business without any smart-alec line. I had a lot to learn.

But she was patient with Tigger.

I did not know what was going to happen. I had been alone with my girl in the orchard, in her grandmother's house once, in my parents' kitchen for a while, but never like this, miles from anyone, unless there should be a sudden parent at the door. That thought made me edgy at first, and slightly panicked later on.

Well, you know — kissing. I loved the feel of her thinness against my chest. I put my arms around her, and enjoyed the scent of her hair. I thought to myself: if I ever have to describe this in a story or a poem I will not be able to do it. I felt her thigh against mine and pressed back as slightly as I could. She opened her mouth and breathed on me, that breath I knew. I'd read somewhere that breath is the soul making itself known, but all I knew was the singularity of Wendy's breath. My right hand was at the small of her back, and her blouse had come untucked from her skirt without any help from me. My fingers felt her smooth skin and the one little bump I knew was there, a kind of freckle that stuck out. I always looked for it, and in the summer I had kissed it.

Stupid, eh? This is what I was like, an inexpert youth filled with desire, trying to keep my self-regard on a secret cultured level. I had tumult in my pants, and I was of two minds about it. Not really minds, you understand. I was sitting on the couch and she was sitting on my lap and kissing my throat. Autumn afternoon light had come around the blinds to find a place in the room.

Do you remember the skirts high school girls wore in those days? I'm pretty sure that I've mentioned Wendy's. You could see a bit of calf and then white bobby socks folded over, and either girls' penny loafers or saddle oxfords. Those socks and shoes went with the other kind of skirt too, a plaid, usually in dark greens and blues, usually pleated, wrapped around and kept together with an outsized safety pin. Both kinds of skirts were tight at the rump, and there was a lovely slope from waist to rump that you made sure to palm when you were at dancing class.

Wendy was wearing a tweed skirt that she could not have run away in, it was so long and so narrow. But it had a zipper in the back that would not stay all the way up. I took that as a sign that her family was not well off. Others might have seen it as a sign of restlessness at least. I always put the best light on things in those days. But I did see to it that the zipper came all the way down. While I kissed her the buttons of her white shirt all came undone, and there was her little brassiere. I had seen the word "bra" in magazines, but I didn't know how to say it. And the word "brassiere" was too awkward. I pushed the shirt down off her right shoulder and then I kissed her neck and shoulder. Now I could hear her breath, and I stopped wondering about her soul.

I think that she arced her back in such a way that we shared in the removing of her shirt. Things were moving awfully fast for me. I reached and took her fallen shirt and folded it awkwardly, then tossed it onto the nearby chair. I wondered whether I was supposed to be undoing my own shirt buttons. I didn't want to do anything of which she would disapprove. If she were to undo one button, I would help with the rest. If she even played with the top button, I would help.

Meanwhile there was the brassiere. It was a little thing, and I easily opened it with one hand, then while she awkwardly raised her arms, took it and tossed it toward the chair. Then I held her against me, awkwardly there on the couch. I leaned back, and through my shirt I could feel her breast upon me. It sounds crazy, but with my hands on her bare back I thought of the words "trunk" and "torso." I thought of "bust" and felt my face flush.

We fell over sideways, and I started with her skirt, and that was difficult. It meant that I was really aiming to remove her clothing. There would be no confusion about whether it was an accident. But she helped me a very little bit, raising her hips, perhaps, as I pulled downward, and touching my hand with complicity as I got the tweed over her heel. Her shoes were on the floor — it would be years till I asked a woman to keep her shoes on. I took her socks, and god help me, I held each one to my nose before tossing it toward the chair.

And there.

In the faint October light.

She was lying on her back with nothing on but her plain panties. I took my time approaching them, not because I was an artful lover but because I was a frightened boy. Her skin was cool to my fingertips and fingernails, but I felt as if I were burning up. My fingers must have felt hot on her skin. I felt that I was expected to proceed, so I did, slowly, moving the imperfect elastic waist down, past the sudden light pubic hair, down her straight lovely thighs, and this time she had not only lifted her hips a little, but bent her feet, one by one, so that I could silently, without a word or even a breath, remove the faint cloth and throw it toward the chair.

I will never forget this, I said inside my head.

We did not say any words to one another. It was totally quiet there beside the lake. Though it was early October, the air in the dark little house was only slightly chilly. Wendy lay naked and white on her back on the couch, and I sat on the floor's thin carpet beside her. She almost gleamed there in the semi-darkness, her eyes closed, her hair swept back from her high forehead.

I thought she must be able to hear my heart banging inside its cage. I had read about that in novels, but here it was, happening to me. I heard Wendy's breath, and waited — I was not ready to touch her yet. She raised her long slender arms and I saw the faint light on them. She held her arms above her head, and I heard her breathing. Her small nipples were raised. I took her hands in mine and held them against my face, half-rising from the floor. I kissed her closed eyelids and then kissed her open mouth.

Am I going to? No, I can't. She wants me to. She will let me do anything. We are in love with one another. She has been brought to this, this nakedness, her breath in the quiet. Am I a failure again if I quit now?

But I only kissed her, only kissed her and felt her body. I did not lie down beside her. I did not remove my clothing. Thinking back, I expect that if she had touched me I would have continued, however awkwardly, however frightened. Ah, I could not take advantage of her, I explained to myself. But really, was it just that I was too frightened?

I kissed her nipples and kissed her between her small breasts and put my hand on her thigh. She would let me do whatever we wanted. But I only kissed her, and I almost released in my trousers. But then I held her without moving, and soon she gently rose and put her brassiere on, and I told her I loved her.

"I love you too, Tigger," she said. She had got her breath back.

CHAPTER 17

IT WAS ALWAYS romantic and noble, my long innocent affair with Wendy Love. That afternoon in my mother's shack, before we walked hand in hand back to town was the only occasion upon which I saw her with all her clothes off. I touched her breasts and put my hand tentatively between her legs on occasion, but she never put her hand on my groin. When I was in grade seven I was not certain what the word groin meant. I was always reading about ballplayers who had groin injuries. I remember deciding that the groin must be that area between your neck and your shoulder. Wendy kissed me there from time to time.

It was always romantic. I always acted as if the cameras were rolling. I didn't change much as I stumbled into adult life. Three engagements later I took to smashing walls with my fist, until I hit a concrete wall with burlap pasted to it. Still, having your hand and arm in a cast again was kind of romantic. I think it was because of the fiancée before that one that I decided to jump from a bridge on a rainy night, and somehow my friend Lionel found out about it and stopped his Morris Minor on the bridge and took me to his tiny house to dry off and have some soup.

I think I have told those two stories. Maybe not. But there they are to verify this and that. Regarding Wendy and our on-again off-again love affair, with the stress on the love, I will relate what happened a few years after the events I have been describing. I realize that such flash-forwards tend to stick out like a sore thumb or other body part in a memoir such as this, but just this once I want to tell this story, because, damn it, I now know for a certainty that there were no cameras on the scene at the time. And if God saw me, which I thought possible at the time, he is not going to bother showing anyone that movie.

High schools are a lot different now than ours was then. In those days each school had a school song. I still remember ours, composed as it was by Gar McKinley, our music and band teacher. I also remember the Penticton High School song, which used a tune from some big US university fight song. Nowadays if you ask a high-schooler about his school song, he has no idea what you are talking about. And as to music and band teachers — in our day you were in the choir and the band as part of your extracurricular activities, like being in the school plays or writing for the school paper. Nowadays high school students get credit for band or choir, and probably for plays.

Grade twelve was a lot different then, too. We had our graduation ceremony in the school auditorium and the dance in the school gym. Nowadays the graduating class spends hundreds of dollars on costumes, and limousines, and the ceremonies, and dances at expensive downtown hotels. The school is dark while the kids and teachers sit in their funny clothes and listen to endless clichés under the bright chandelier at the Sheraton.

At Southern Okanagan High School a lot of the guys got school rings and school sweaters. You don't see school sweaters anymore either, except maybe in *Archie* comics. Our sweater was a green cardigan with yellow stripes around the upper sleeves. Upon this you would ask your mother to sew the felt crests you won for athletics or arts or school service or good grades. Nowadays the kids get checks. My sweater had a lot of green and gold crests on it, and it went back and forth. Wendy wore it for quite a while, and I was proud as could be to see her wearing my sweater around school and elsewhere. She gave it back to me once or twice. I don't know where it wound up.

But I sort of know where my class ring wound up the summer after high school and before we went to Victoria for college (George) and normal school (Wendy). Cranna's jewelry store downtown made good business on school rings. The guys in grade twelve would get a ring with sohs and the year displayed in green and gold, as in gold the colour. There might have been some gold metal involved, too, I think. I, being creative and romantic, took my ring back to Cranna's and had some special engraving done on the side where the ring was getting wide enough to have the letters and numbers on the front. I had wl engraved on one side, and gb engraved on the other side. We got these rings early in the spring term, and wore them through the last months of grade twelve. For all of April I wore the ring. Then I gave it to Wendy, and we knew that this was either a symbol or a cliché, and she wore it on a chain around her neck.

I am not going to tell you all the details of our romantic heart-rending breakup, because this is a flash-forward, but I can tell you that breaking up was Wendy's idea. We would break up again after most of a year in Victoria, and yet again a year or so further on, when I was in the air force and she was at university. Suffice it to say that this first time, when I was seventeen, I would have jumped off a bridge if there had been one high enough within walking distance of Oliver. Well, there were cliffs, but I was afraid of cliffs unless I was climbing them.

She gave me back my ring. She did not throw it at my feet, and she did not scream and tear her hair while handing it over. She just put it down on an open page of the book I was reading at the time, *The Moon and Sixpence* by Somerset Maugham. The book was about as romantic as you can get — the guy becomes a painter and runs away to Tahiti, where he ends his life blind with leprosy, frantically painting his last works without seeing them, ordering his native woman to burn them when he has died. I just knew I had to be an artist and suffer and eat very little and perish unknown. And then Wendy dropped our ring on the page.

At the time I thought Somerset Maugham was a first-rate literary author, like James M. Cain.

All right, to make a long flash-forward short, I did not get drunk, because I had just graduated from high school, but I went for one of my sullen hikes. If you were going on a hike around Oliver in those days, you went up the hills on the west side or you went up the hills on the east side. If you were doing the latter you were in Indian country, which was a lot easier then than it is now that the Okanagan people have learned to be political. In those days you might even go and fool around in Manuel Louie's barn. Once a few years earlier Manuel Louie, who was the chief in those days, had caught us in his barn and demanded to know our names.

"Will Trump," I said.

"George Bowering," piped up Will.

And when we went down the hill toward home, we said tee-hee behind our hands, we'd sure fooled him.

But this night, when I saw Manuel Louie's barn ahead of me, I turned to my right, leaving the dirt road and walking south along the sagebrush bench overlooking the Okanagan River and the dusty town that bordered it. It was some time between nine and ten at night, so the sun had gone behind a mountain on the other side, and blazing daylight had been replaced by a kind of silver light that hung on the edges of tumbleweed and sagebrush. In the daytime you knew enough to watch the ground in front of you, where cactuses probably were and rattlesnakes might be. When the sun goes behind the mountain the air begins to cool and rocks remain warm, so snakes like to warm their blood by coiling on them.

I didn't care. I headed for the trees. The trees on the bench were closer together than they were along most of this side, some as close together as a hundred and fifty feet. I probably stepped on cactuses. I did not even listen for snakes. The grasshoppers had shut up an hour ago, and it was past bedtime for frogs along the river. It was so quiet that I could hear my breath. I thought that I could hear the blood in the veins alongside my head.

This is about as romantic as it gets, I must have thought. This is a defining moment in the story of my life. The fact that there are no cameras will just etch this moment into my memory the way those initials are etched into the goldish sides of this ring.

I had twisted it off my left ring finger and now held it in my right hand. There are no cameras because this is not a movie; this is a book, my life. Don't forget this. Save it. I turned the way a discus thrower turns, and flung that ring as far as I could into the dark air, so far that I could not hear it, so far that if I ever changed my mind I could never find it in a hundred years, much less fifty-four. By the time I walked away from that spot there were a million stars in the black sky, and I was ready to leave the valley forever.

I wonder whether a metal detector ...? No. No.

*S*PILL, MEMORY.

That's a little reference for the erudite who'll think they know what's going on. There's another one later on.

On the first day of school Jeanette MacArthur did not show up. Oh no, not again, I thought. What I was referring to inside my own head was the first day of school in grade five. In grade four I had fallen in love with Janie Richmond, a girl who had moved up from Red Bluff, California. She was an incredibly beautiful brunette nine-or-ten-year-old, my first USAmerican girl. The year I was in grade four we had a population explosion of kids, so two classes had to meet at the old Scout Hall, a big brown wooden building in a huge lot down the hill from the elementary school. Now that I picture it, I think it must have been a school long before the newer and bigger school was built on the hill.

Except when we played anti-aye-over with the Scout Hall roof, it was tacitly or advisedly agreed that the girls were to play on the south side and the boys on the north side. Halfway through the winter I started hanging out on the girls' side, playing their games, though I did not stoop to jacks in the spring. What we mainly did was to run through town, though never down to the main street, hollering and laughing.

Is this a confession of some sort?

Anyway, I did not see Janie Richmond during the summer between grade four and grade five. I didn't have a job yet, just chores around my place, and around my grandparents' place in Summerland while I was up there for a few weeks. I was excited as a boy can be on the first morning of the new school year in grade five, and then I was smacked between the eyebrows by the shocking news that the Richmonds had moved back to California.

For years after that, for decades, I would make Will laugh by sighing and saying "Janie" in a drawn-out plaint.

I visited Red Bluff, California with my daughter in around 1983, and casually looked around for a beautiful brunette in her late forties. Twenty years later my wife Jean and I stayed over-night in a motel in Red Bluff. Not only did it not look at all like the memory I had of it during my earlier drive through; the Red Bluff and area phone book didn't have any Richmonds in it. There were some brunettes in town, but they were all too young.

So oh, no, not again, I thought, and thought again, for three days. I could have moseyed up to, say, Katie Eisenhut and asked her whether she knew anything about Jeanette MacArthur, but then she would have told Sylvia Macintosh that I was interested in Jeanette, and Sylvia would have told Joan Roberts, and so on.

But on the Monday of the second week, there she was, in a skirt and blouse that were new-looking but probably home-made. On her right arm she was wearing a cast, and around the edge of her right eye was the purple and orange relic of a black eye. I did not see her talking to anyone all day. In social studies class she tried to take notes with her left hand. I wanted to go to her and make up for the fact that no one else was talking to her, but I chickened out. I didn't keep all the rules set by my peers, as parents were always calling them, but some I did, and this was one of them, vague as it was.

It was not till Wednesday that I waited for her at the bridge. She was walking with her head down as usual, but I knew that she was aware of me. She was holding her binder and a couple of textbooks against her chest with her cast. There were no signatures or clever remarks written on it as there would have been for just about anyone else. She was wearing the same skirt and blouse that she had been wearing on Monday.

She made a point of deviating from her path in order to walk around me. I caught up to her and fell into step.

"You going to the post office?" she murmured.

"I could be at that," I said, chipper as could be.

"Correspondence from the moron club?"

"I expect a letter from Ernest Hemingway, asking for advice."

"I have a bit of advice for you," she said. She had not yet looked in my direction, though I was close enough to hit with a textbook.

"Can I sniff your cast? I had a cast on my arm two years ago, and the smell got better and better with each passing day."

I was trying to cheer her up, in a kind of aggressively stupid way, I knew.

"When I get it off I will give it to you," she said. She stopped walking and turned to face me at last. "You can take it to bed with you and hold it in your arms and sniff it all night."

I could feel my face tingling. She sneered and started walking again.

And I had to let her go. For about five seconds a picture of her in bed with me with her arm in a cast began to interfere with my regular thinking, but I fought it off, or I let it go. I watched her walk down the hill in the dust beside the paved road, waiting for her to turn and look back. I said in my sorry head that if she turned back and looked we would be friends, the kind of friends I wanted us to be, but she did not look back once, and I admired her for that.

That night I went creeping around her house by the river again, George Burrowing, master agent. I had done all my chores before supper, and after supper I finished the math homework I had not been able to finish in French class. I listened to an episode of "Tombstone Bogardus: Scourge of the West," on my radio. I drew a few panels of my comic strip "Sam Shovel: Private Eye, Ear, Nose and Throat."

I waited for it to get moderately dark. Daylight Saving Time was hanging on by its fingernails. I put my pile of *Sport* magazines in chronological order. I went around the house and emptied all the ashtrays into an old coffee can. I read one chapter of *The Weapon Shops of Isher* by A.E. van Vogt. This was before I knew that A.E. van Vogt was a Canadian, from a Mennonite town in Manitoba.

Finally, it got dusky enough, and out I slipped into my old hightop sneakers, black with a white star over the ankle bump. I stopped at Frank's pool hall, picked up a Sweet Marie chocolate bar for survival rations, and yucked it up on my way into the back room where the tables were. This way Frank would provide me with an alibi, just in case. I went out the back door and turned right, headed for Sawmill Road.

My shoes crunched on gravel. Machines in the packing house and the cannery and the juice plant and the box factory had gone quiet for the night. There was the occasional truck up on the highway, gearing down as it became Main Street. I heard a woman's loud laughter from a shack among the toolies. A little acid pain made itself known in my stomach. For less than a second the image of Jeanette naked except for an arm cast flitted behind my eyes. But no, no for a certainty, that was not what I was interested in when I was interested in Jeanette. I wanted to know whether it would seem all right for me to want to protect her if I could. I was not thinking of a reward. Along with everything else, I was still a personal voluntary Christian boy in secret, trying to do mysterious good and disappear without a sign.

She hadn't even offered an explanation. Surely, when a girl appears at school after the summer vacation with a cast on her arm, someone will ask her what happened. I didn't have the nerve to, but surely someone would, some less complicated person. Maybe a teacher. She would have had to tell a teacher if the teacher asked, wouldn't she? I supposed that no one had asked. That, it struck me as I crunched gravel alongside Sawmill Road, was sad.

In my head, as was my private custom, I was an anonymously heroic secret agent behind the lines, looking for an angry fox. Not knowing who he was made my job harder and more worthwhile, nearly enjoyable. I stepped into the tall couchgrass beside the road, bringing the crunching to a sudden stop. I stood still, straining to hear anyone who might be straining to hear me.

It was as quiet as can be. The river slid by without a sound.

I could barely hear myself step further down into the weeds, headed for the water, planning to come to Jeanette's house from the side and then the back. It had been months since I'd been crouching around there. The Sweet Marie was melting in my shirt pocket. When I got to Jeanette's house there was a light in the kitchen but nowhere else. I stood up straight in order to look for her.

I heard a sudden intake of breath, so I turned to look into the illuminated greenery behind me, but something — a baseball bat, a lead pipe, a two-by-four smashed into the arm I had put in front of my face. A voice pronounced most of the unpleasant words I knew. I was on my face in the wet weeds, my left hand holding my right arm.

"The fuck out of here," said the dark shape above me.

I moved for a while on my knees. Then I got up somehow and felt my way back to the road and headed for home, holding my arm. I wanted to kneel down again but I was afraid I wouldn't be able to get back up. I walked all the way home, and got inside the house without my parents' seeing me. They were in the kitchen playing cribbage. I had pissed in the yard, so I went straight to my bedroom and lay on the bed without turning on the light or taking off my clothes.

I lay on my back with pain possessing my arm from the shoulder to the fingers. Then shock put me to sleep.

WHEN I WOKE at six in the morning the pain was different. It felt as if I were being held in some other world, where pain had replaced air. My shirt was smeared with chocolate and peanuts. I was sitting at the kitchen table with my right arm hanging from my shoulder when my parents found me.

"Fell down in the dark," I said.

My parents were not the type to get all excited and try to yank the truth out of me. My mother walked with me up the short roadway to the hospital, because my father had to get ready for school.

"Where?"

"Down a hole. Fell off the plank," I said, and then they took me to the operating room and got me to count backward from a hundred by threes. I was pretty good at that, because that's the sort of thing I always did before going to sleep at night. Think of cities that start with M and so on. I think I remember getting back to eighty-eight.

My mother picked me up in the car at noon and drove four blocks to get us the one block distance. I was glad she had done so.

"Where was this hole?" she asked after the second left turn.

"Someone's back yard. Shortcut I used to take."

"Well, I hope you've learned a lesson," she told me, plunking some Campbell's tomato soup in front of me when we got home.

"Can I go to school this afternoon?"

"Tomorrow."

⌒

SO I BEGAN my days as a left-handed demi-hero in the narrative unfolding inside my cranium. When people asked me what had happened to my arm I was evasive. I'd say "accident" or "fell down a hole" or "plain rotten luck," or once in a while "defending democracy." But no matter how curious my friends and enemies were, I did not offer any details. When Bob Fleming, our mercurial math teacher noticed two arm casts in one class he got off a pretty good one.

"I heard you were both raking leaves and fell out of a tree," he said. Then he did some logarithms on the blackboard.

I turned my head and looked back at Jeanette, but she was looking down at her math book, I guess. I was pretty good at math, even left-handed. Mr. Fleming did not make me write on the board, but he did ask me a question and I did answer it pretty well, even slipping in a little comic repartee.

Being a teenaged boy, I was pretty clumsy to start with, but I was really made aware of my clumsiness with a cast on my arm. I banged it against every hard surface I came near. I wore my jacket on my left arm and shoulder, thinking how noble I must look. Inside the cast my broken radius really did hurt, despite the aspirins in my system. That was all right — I had a kind of fond relationship with pain. Some of you will know what I mean.

In the late afternoon I had a study period, and so did Jeanette. In study hall you could sit wherever you wanted to. I managed to sit two rows to her right, and after a few minutes of applying ballpoint to paper, I managed to print, "If you tell me how you broke yours I'll tell you how I broke mine." I got Len Lavik, who was sitting between us, to pass her the note.

When her note came back I saw that she could write left-handed far better than I could. I was surprised to see that she had replied at all. I took this as a good sign. Here is what she wrote: "I can't read your scrawl. Was it something about Australia?"

I passed another note to Len Lavik. He looked at me and gestured, and we traded desks. Of course I dropped two or three things in the process, then banged my cast loudly on the desk-top while trying to gather everything, and all in all caught the attention of Mr. Raeburn the woodworking teacher who was supervising study hall, so that by the time I got into my new seat between Len Lavik and Jeanette MacArthur, Jeanette was not there any more, having gathered up her stuff quietly, despite having an arm in a cast, and moved to a spare desk up front. I asked Len for my note back but he said he didn't have it. That was not good news, because the note read: "I got mine in your back yard. Where did you get yours?" One could only hope that the note would get lost in the general shuffling of feet, but I was not putting any money on that.

CHAPTER 19

As you know, in those days arm casts were heavy, and the arms inside them got hot and sweaty and itchy. I undid a wire coat hanger and used it to poke up inside and scratch as well as I could. Another thing those casts would get is smelly. There is a certain smell that could be nothing else but the scent you get when you put your nose at the end of your arm cast. Well, it probably applies to leg casts as well, but I could never get my nose next to the leg casts I have managed to earn over a lifetime of clumsiness.

But you can't stop sniffing. The odour is not really what most people would call pleasant. I like the smell of lemons, and I am a big fan of pine needles, but I have to say that I could not keep my nose away from the opening at the thumb end of my cast. I did not do the usual teen thing and get all my classmates to write clever sayings on it, but I did offer them a sniff. I remember that Leo Smith took me up on the offer and made the requisite face and oral response. Joe Makse took a whiff and approved, of course, because he knew that I would do the same thing for him. And naturally Will had a shot at it every day, announcing the progress it had made. My mother would not even give it a try. As an inducement, I offered her my beets at dinner one night, and she still would not do it.

I had thought, speaking of my mother, that the broken arm and the clumsy cast would get me out of my daily chores, but I was to learn differently. All that happened was that my daily tasks took me longer to do. Bringing in the wood and kindling wasn't all that hard, because I just stacked them on my cast, though it was a little awkward, because I was used to stacking them on my left arm. The sawdust took longer because it isn't easy filling a tall bucket with sawdust when you are using one and a half arms. I could still use the fingers of my right hand, but my thumb was not opposable as it had been billed to be in Grade Seven science.

So no matter how I tried, I could not use a pool cue properly. I tried shooting left-handed, but had trouble hitting the cue ball straight on. So I hung out in Frank's pool hall, shooting the shit with the other boys trying to act old enough to be legal. Sometimes ten of us crammed into and onto Ordie Jones's car and went down there for our forty-minute lunch hour. We were also likely to be there or across the street at the Orchard Cafe pool room after school.

Frank's poolroom was pretty neat. It had the sense of having been there on the main strip in Oliver since olden days, what with its oiled wooden floor that creaked when you walked across it. Frank was a skinny old coot with a suit vest on over a shirt. He was some kind of uncle to Joe Makse or maybe John Jalovec, one of those Jugoslavians anyway. He was always in conversation with some other old Jugoslavian or German guy. He sat on a stool behind his counter where the cigarettes and cigars were, and surveyed his estate. Between this large front room and the steps down to the poolroom was Hector Povich's glassed-in haircut place, one chair, some waiting. Hector Povich had one leg a lot shorter than the other, and a shoe with an eight-inch sole. He leaned on you or the chair while he was flashing his scissors, and he always pointed at us underage kids with them. I got my haircuts at home.

When you came in the door off the street and headed for Frank's counter or the steps down to the pool hall, you'll remember, you walked past the magazine and "pocketbook" racks. I didn't call them pocketbooks, unless they were published by Pocket Books, being a teenaged snob. I liked to keep track of the brands: Pocket Books, Bantam Books, I remember, the New American Library (Signet), Dell Books, Gold Medal Books, White Circle Books, Popular Library. I still feel a little surge of excitement now, just reciting these names. I bought *Sport Life* magazine there, the second-best sports mag. And you'll remember that I bought my first poetry book here, that being Damon Runyan's *Poems for Men* (Permabooks, 1951, 35 cents). "Over 100 virile, roistering ballads about guys and dolls by the guy who knew 'em best of all."

That was my connection to the big city, right there in that hick town pool hall. And not just New York. My sports authors (as opposed to just sportswriters) had grown to include Shirley Povich in Washington, Bob Broeg in St. Louis, Hal Lebovitz in Cleveland, and the white-haired man who was always called the "Dean" of sportswriters, Grantland Rice. I thought that Granny Rice was pretty well going to be my favourite writer for a long time. I thought he was just plain grander than, say, Max Brand, my favourite book writer.

While working in a bowling alley was all right as far as small town Christian morality was concerned, at least in our town, just being in a pool hall was getting close to juvenile delinquency, a popular phrase of the time. I don't know, all these years later, whether my father was ever in a pool hall or a beer parlour. Of course the latter was an unlikely place to be for a schoolteacher in a two-beer-parlour town. I thought that Damon Runyan had a beer sometimes, though, and I figured that he knew his way around a pool hall. He wrote about the racetrack too, a place that was sort of for sports and sort of for racketeers.

"You interested in buying that pocketbook or reading it over the duration of a month?"

This was Frank, who fixed me with a sardonic look. Sardonic was one of my favourite words that year, along with formidable.

"Just checking to see if I have read it," I said.

"That's whether."

"Just checking to see whether I have read it."

Another reason for hanging out at Frank's. He did not correct other kids' grammar, except maybe for Joe's or John's, whichever was his nephew.

If he were still around today, I would lend him this badge. He helped me earn it.

I plunked down a little row of coins on his glass top counter, and headed out the door carrying my shiny copy of *Startling Stories* with a story by Leigh Brackett in it. It would be another thirty years before I knew that Leigh Brackett was a woman.

I was slowly placing one foot in front of the other along the sidewalk while reading the first paragraphs of Leigh Brackett's story, when I felt fingers grip my left biceps. I stopped walking and read to the end of the sentence before looking to see who had a hold of me. It was Miss Verge, standing beside a tree in an earthen pot. The tree and Miss Verge were of equal height.

Here was the idea: being a hale young man, I was to help Miss Verge get this youthful tree up the stairs and into her apartment. I was a noble lad, as I have told you, yet at the same time I experienced a reluctant horniness. I folded *Startling Stories* and put it into the back pocket of my brown corduroys.

I was a teenaged boy. According to newspaper stories about scientific reports in more recent years, I was thinking about sex three times a minute. In fact, while I had been in Frank's pool hall, even while I was looking at the magazines and paperbacks, I had been thinking about a dream I had had a week ago, a dream that I thought about several times a day.

It seems that I had fainted at my desk during Social Studies class, which was too bad, because we had been studying the Battle of Hastings, and I was crazy about the Battle of Hastings. I would flinch and breathe fast when I thought about getting a Norman arrow in my eye. It was not at all clear that Harold should have been king, but it was not all that clear that William should have been, either. Poor Harold, he had just defeated a Norwegian invasion led in part by his brother, and now here he was at the south coast with an arrow in his eye. Maybe I fainted thinking of that.

In any case, I woke up, it seems, lying on my back on the cot-like bed in the nurse's room next to the principal's office. I woke with a thin blanket on me, pulled up to my chin. I felt a little funny, but of course you would feel a little funny waking up in the nurse's room. Then the nurse entered the room and closed the door behind her. She bent down to ask me how I was feeling, and because she had the top two buttons of her starched white nurse's shirt undone, afforded me a generous glimpse of her lovely round breasts. Notice that I say breasts, because that was such a horny word for them in those days.

And she stayed bent over, asking me questions in a semi-whisper.

"Do you still feel faint?"

"Are you warm enough with that blanket?"

"Would you like a glass of water?"

"Do you feel feverish?"

Every time I started to answer one of her questions, she would ask another. At last, after enquiring about a fever, she placed her cool hand on my forehead. I felt as if I had a fever, as if her cool hand was all I required to bring me back to health.

Then, as if all that bending over was putting a strain on her body, she let herself down on her knees.

"Do you often faint like that?"

"Is there a history of fainting in your family?"

Two more buttons had come undone. She was wearing nothing under her crisp white shirt. One of her beautiful breasts was almost out.

The small hand on my forehead still felt cool, but now I felt her other hand, and it was warm. It had made its way beneath the thin blanket, and was now on my flat bare midriff. Of course, she had loosened my clothing because I had fainted. They always did that in novels.

I was not really hearing her questions now, just a kind of buzz nearby. I think the blood was leaving my head and going elsewhere. I felt the nurse's soft lips on my mouth and a few seconds later the tip of her tongue on mine. Her hand was now on my stiffened pecker, which was tangled in my jockey shorts. She gently worked it loose, and it was lying on my belly. I did not kiss her in return. I did not reach for one of the bare breasts that hung before me. The hand that had been on my forehead was now in my hair, and the other grasped my cock, which had been jumping on my belly. She kissed me and spoke into my mouth as she moved her warm hand with its sure grip up and down my teen boy penis.

Then I woke up and I was indeed lying on my back, but in my own little bed, with something warm on my belly, something that turned cool and slid down my side.

As I said, I remembered that dream, and every night for a week

I had been trying to get back into it. The school nurse was Leoni Dexter, I remember, not as gorgeous as the nurse in my dream, but I took to imagining her instead of trying to name every player in the National Hockey League as I was waiting in my little bed for sleep. While waiting I held myself as much like a nurse as I could manage. But the dream was taking its time in returning. At school I went out of my way to walk past the nurse's station several times a day, hoping to prime the pump, so to speak. I hung around the drinking fountain across the hall from her door. Occasionally I saw her, in an unsatisfying quick passage. I contemplated faking a faint, but I didn't have the nerve.

Now here I was helping Miss Verge carry a heavy plant up a long flight of stairs. Well, it was not all that heavy. I could have carried it myself, even with my right arm in a cast. In fact, it passed through my mind that Miss Verge could have carried it up herself. If not, I wondered, how had she managed to get it to the sidewalk in front of her stairway door?

Nevertheless, I did break into a sweat on the way up those steps. I was wearing ordinary early October duds, a Hawaiian shirt with my father's off-white cardigan over it, the right sleeve hanging, and my brown cords. I had sweat in my hair above my ears, and a bead or two on my forehead. I may as well have been setting pins.

"Here, let's put it in front of the window," said Miss Verge, breathing a little heavily. She was wearing her typical early October teacher's clothes, a navy blue skirt that showed her slightly thick legs from just below the knees, a light blue blouse that could have been made of silk, with a maroon blazer over it. Her black hair had become a little undone on the way upstairs. Her blouse was a little untucked on one side. I have always liked that for some reason.

I felt my face blushing or flushing or whatever that was called. I thought of turning and running downstairs. But I was in a space I remembered with some confusion. My thing was heavy and a little swollen, hanging down my right thigh the way it did when I was dancing with Lois Robin.

"I think about you sometimes," said Miss Verge, in her school-teacher voice.

"Uh ...," I managed to say.

"Do you think of me sometimes?"

Her chest touched my upper left arm. I mean I could feel it through my sweater and shirt.

"Sometimes, yes," I said.

Her chest moved but stayed touching the upper sleeve of my sweater. I felt my cock trying to rise in the front of my cords. Miss Verge noticed.

"Look," she said, dropping her eyes.

I did not have to look to know, but I looked, and I saw my cords sticking out in front. When Miss Verge took my sweater off me, I hardly noticed. It was really warm in that apartment over the Food Basket. I hardly noticed when her blazer joined my sweater on the Oriental rug.

"I ...," I managed to utter.

I was woozy on my feet or something. All the blood had left my head. I tried to take a step toward the couch. Miss Verge held my hips in her hands, preventing any such move.

"I want you to stay standing," she said.

And she touched the bump in my pants. It leapt at her.

She reached for my belt, and as she undid it, she gradually bent in front of me, ending up on her knees. My cords fell all the way down, and now my jockey shorts stuck out in front of me.

"Wait," she said, and stood up quickly.

"Don't move," she said.

I stayed still, except for the part that was now poking out above the weak elastic of my jockey shorts.

Miss Verge came back from wherever she had been. She was still wearing her high heels and her clothes, but her shirt was open all the way, and her brassiere had disappeared.

"Take this," she said, and handed me a thick little book. I took it in my left hand. She resumed her place in front of me, kneeling and running her hands up my legs. She reached around behind me and felt my bum. I was worried about possible pimples, but soon stopped worrying. My jockey shorts were now at my ankles.

"Open it and read," she said, her voice mainly breath.

"Oh, Jesus," I said, in response to the touch I felt under my scrotum.

"Have you read anything about the Dionysian rites?" she asked.

"No, I —"

"Open anywhere and read out loud."

I managed with one and a half hands. What the hell is this, I asked myself. It's scary, I told myself. But I read out loud:

> *Dogmatic Teachers, of the snow-white fur!*
> *Ye wrangling Schoolmen, of the scarlet hood!*
> *Who, with a keenness not to be —*

One hand was cupping my nuts and the other was holding my shaft and moving up and down in a pumping motion I knew well though not with another's hand. I could not believe how vertical my cock was.

"Read," she said.

> *Who, with a keenness not to be withstood,*
> *Press the point home, or falter and demur,*

Checked in your course by many a teasing burr;
Oh, god, oh my god —

I could not see her because I was holding the book in both hands, more or less, but I knew, I knew it, my cock was in her mouth.

"Nnnr's nn uhh."

"What?"

"There's no oh my gods in that poem," she said, and then again took me in, and now moved her mouth and let me know about her tongue.

These natural council-seats your acrid blood
Might cool; — and, as the Genius of the flood
Stoops willingly to animate and spur

"Oh, please," I said, almost dropping the book, bending my knees just a little. She sucked slowly once and moved her head back so that I could see her past the book, shaking her hair off her forehead.

"The sestet, please," she said, and her face disappeared.

I don't think that my hips were moving in anything like iambics.

Each lighter function slumbering in the brain,
Yon eddying balls of foam

She giggled, it felt like, with her mouth full.

Yon eddying balls of foam, these arrowy gleams
That o'er the pavement of the surging streams
Welter and flash, a sy—, a sy—, sy—

"Synod," she said, and now she bent further and touched her pointed tongue to my balls of foam.

> *Welter and flash, a synod might detain*
> *With subtle speculations, haply vain,*
> *But surely less so than your far-fetched themes!*

I dropped the book onto the rug where it disappeared without a sound. I put my left hand on Miss Verge's head, and spouted all over her face and hair and over her head somewhere. She put me back into her mouth and sucked hard. I had never felt so good in my short life. I thought an angel might hack me with a sword on my way down the stairs.

Miss Verge looked up at me with a big smile and wide open eyes, and then she licked her lips. I had to close my eyes. I didn't quite believe all this then. My knees could hardly hold me up. Finally Miss Verge took me by the arm with a cast on it and led me to her couch, where I sat down heavily. I closed my eyes.

And Wendy appeared, her small bare breasts filmed with perspiration.

I opened my eyes, and saw Miss Verge going into the bathroom. I stood and did my buttons up. It took a while, which I blamed on my arm cast. Now what, I asked myself. What am I supposed to do now?

I was still standing, irresolute, when Miss Verge came out of the bathroom, her hair a little wild but her clothing all in place, though I could tell that she had nothing on under her shirt.

"Here," she said, "Be careful on the stairs."

I walked in a daze.

"And here," she said. "Take the book with you. Read some more, and think about what you read."

"Yes."

"And where have you been?"

"Uh."

"You have been wasting your time in the pool hall. You could have been doing your homework."

"I have done all my homework."

"And still you have so much to learn," said Miss Verge.

CHAPTER *20*

I COULDN'T SET pins with my arm in a cast, and I was surprised by how much I missed it, at least for the teachers' league. There was a kind of camaraderie among the teachers, in which no one made anything of the wide range of their bowling skills. And I felt as if I were on the outer parts of their circle, kind of a pet pinsetter. I was "Ewart's boy," of course, and this bowling business was not the only occasion on which I got to see the lives of the school-teachers from inside. They helped build each other's houses, for example, and when they were working on our place, I shovelled sand and gravel and cement into the mixer along with Bob Fleming, the ambidextrous mathematics teacher. We knew that he was ambidextrous, because he had a habit of spinning from the blackboard and firing pieces of chalk at noise-makers, and you never knew which way he was going to come 'round.

I didn't miss my regular league pin setting as much. I definitely did not miss being within firing range of Ritchie Schneider's cannon ball. But I even went down and watched the teachers bowling, though I was not going to go home with my dollar and

210 • GEORGE BOWERING

a half. On those occasions I had to watch the art teacher and Miss Verge from behind the seats, so there was no question of looking up their skirts. I made sure to avoid eye contact with Miss Verge, and paid closer attention to the art teacher. During every frame her shirt would come untucked at the waist, and I could see skin. Once or twice I saw the elastic of her underpants. But that was it — while I had no fantasies about getting anywhere with the art teacher, before coming to the bowling alley I had begun to put some of my sister's white cream stuff on my pimples.

I can't really remember how well-focused my fantasies were. I would remain sort of inexperienced for another five years, so I had no help from memory. In those days there was no hardcore pornography, and you never saw a bare tit in a movie. It wasn't till 1960 that you thought you might have got a half-second glimpse of Capucine's nipple in *North to Alaska*. Till then you had to be satisfied with Jean Simmons in a bonnet and lace collar.

I did like certain items of clothing on the girls in my class. Maybe I wasn't aware of them as fetish material. Maybe I just thought they were, as we would say at the time, neat. White socks and saddle oxfords would come first. They were the neatest and cutest (if I might use a girl's word) items of footwear in history, and footwear has a great history. I didn't care what colour it was that went with the white, but I suppose that if I had my choice, my druthers, as we said back then, I would go for the dark blue. The hot colour for shoes those few years was oxblood. Even I had a pair of oxblood shoes, with dorsal fins on the toes. But saddle oxfords are nothing without white bobby socks. The socks should be folded down once, and they should be white as can be. Sometimes you would see pink ones, or lace trim or even a little cotton bauble, but these were distractions that showed a failure of imagination.

What did the girls wear with these fabulous shoes? I've told you about those long pencil skirts and that other pleated one I favoured, wrapped around and pinned together with a huge safety pin, the bigger the better. I longed to open one of those safety pins but I never did. Wendy didn't have one, for one thing, and for another, I never did get very far with Wendy below the waist.

The girls' clothes of my youth were not as sexy and provocative, as minimal as they are nowadays. Or maybe in those days we thought they were pretty sexy, and maybe nowadays the boys in school aren't moved much by all the bare skin they get to see. Well, yes, and they are spoiled by being able to see people doing all manner of sexual things on their computers. And most movie stars nowadays are shown naked somewhere on the Internet. I don't think I even imagined Deborah Kerr with her clothes off — though I can do it right now. Things have changed — and maybe they have not. When I was fifteen I got a hard on if I looked inside a short sleeve. Or if a girl turned around really fast in a poodle skirt.

A lot of the girls in my class at school made their own clothes, and the clothes they made were a combination of the kind their mothers knew how to make and the clothes they imagined might make them look more like Marilyn Monroe. Meanwhile a lot of the guys wore shirts made by their mothers. I was lucky — my mother would make me a shirt out of any material I chose. I wore the wildest shirts in my class, and sometimes they were even made of curtain material. But I was envious of the guys who had classier shoes and pants.

My best moment came when the fashion was blue draped pants with long maroon blazers. Len Lavik and I were the only two guys who had maroon draped pants with blue blazers. But Sylvia still didn't swoon, and Dummy Rattery's big sister did not push me into a dark closet.

I am looking at a picture of me, grade ten or eleven, on the wall in front of me at this minute. In the picture I'm leaning against the white outside wall of Fred Van Hoorn's house. His baby brother André is looking out the window above my head, the same André Miller who is now a bigwig in the Oliver town government. Beside me is my little brother Roger, about four or five years old, frowning in the sunlight, wearing what looks as if it is probably a brown fuzzy plaid jacket, though the photo is black and white. I am holding and reading a copy of *Pogo* comics. My hair is growing out of a boogie cut — remember those? Long and greasy and combed straight back at the sides to a ducktail in the back, brush cut on top. I seem to have my dad's old brown leather jacket on, under which I am wearing a white shirt with the collar turned up. The pants look like my old brown corduroy drapes, and the cheapo belt is done up clumsily, leaving the waist of the pants hanging over it. It has to be a pose, signifying candid.

My buddy Will's pants always looked as if he were wearing a couple of leg bags tied at the top by a rope. He never did get into the scene with drapes and pocket chains and boogie cuts. My friendship with him was something apart from my being in the rest of the kid world.

Long before developing any highly narrative and pictorial sex fantasies, Will and I had performed a fanciful life. We had been neighbourhood cowboy heroes, dark alley crime busters, interstellar space explorers, language inventors, sword duellists, roamers of clue-infested mystery hills, and inventors. We had been building an airplane for years, writing a movie, and burying treasures in mountain earth on both sides of the valley.

We used our spare time to hone our skill at conversation.

"My aunt Lorna is worried about the thinness of her hair," I would say. "She's looking into buying a perruque."

"No, no, that's a kind of dugout canoe."

"You mean a pirogue."

"Uh uh, that's a Ukrainian dumpling."

"You mean a pyrogy."

"Not at all. That's the mountains between Spain and France."

"Pyrenees! Pyrenees!"

"Dolt!

"I resemble that!"

"Now you're talking about Bedelia Glotenschnaubel. She's got a terrific pair of knees."

As time went on, the conversation would more and more often turn in such a way that we were describing and picturing the bodies of women and girls we were acquainted with. Or if not entire bodies, then at least parts of bodies. Teenaged boys, in those days, became devotees of girls' and women's body parts.

It should be pointed out that girls' and women's body parts were not restricted or confined, let us say, to girls and women. I've mentioned looking out the window of our family car as my father drove the Oliver Bowerings up the valley to visit the Naramata Bowerings, looking forward to a certain little mountain range near Okanagan Falls, because from a certain stretch of Highway 97 this little arête looked like the profile of the firm and sumptuous breasts of two young women lying on their backs. In fact the more I looked, the more I anthropomorphized, or maybe I should say eroticized, the landscape.

Similar imaginative magic was to be worked on illustrations found on food packaging, the secret tits complete with nipples on the orchard scene of the apple box label, for example. Certain trees that I had known since grade three were now voluptuous. Clouds no longer looked like lambs or Africa. Headless mannequins in the window of Henderson's Clothing were targets of my developing lust, and I cursed my bad luck in never being there when they were being undressed.

All this adolescent creativeness was supposed by us to be a sign that we were leaving childhood aside. In fact, this was when one started referring to oneself as a "man."

"I am not much interested in Bedelia Glotenschnaubel's knees," I said, while we patrolled the hill back of Manuel Louie's barn. "I'm a tit man."

Will was watching the ground for rattlesnakes. I had been trying all spring and summer to imitate the sound of a rattlesnake, just so I could make him jump, maybe into a mess of cactuses.

"I don't see it," he said. "I could never be a tit man, though I do understand that at least half the guys I know are."

"Well, I am not completely a tit man," I said. "I could also be described as an ass man. Especially, for example, when it comes to Katie Eisenhut."

"Still don't get it," said Will.

"I'll bet you don't," I said, trying to make him think that I did, I mean in the other sense, but doubting that he would.

I really like putting down all this dialogue, because for some reason I can remember it more exactly than I can the stuff that requires description — people's clothes, the weather, and so on. I don't remember everything that Will was wearing during these conversations, so I might lean toward supplying the *kind* of pants he was wearing, or just not mention them at all. There are some writers, such as James Lee Burke, who can't get into a scene without telling you what the sky looked like or what the characters were wearing. He is very big on colours, especially. But if anyone mentions the woman in the green dress at the party I attended last week, I haven't got a clue.

"I am not an ass man," said Will, "nor am I a tit man, a chin man, a shoulder man, a nose man — I am none of those men."

"You gotta be a something man," I said. "I hope you are not going to give me that guff about liking them for their personality or their soul, or something. Don't disappoint me, Trump."

He was using his thumbnail to try to get a little dab of dried food off his light brown corduroys. Above us the sky was Mediterranean blue, with one little stretched cloud over Mount Baldy.

"I favour kachunga legs," he said at last.

"You're a leg man, then," I said with relief in my voice.

"Not just any legs. You take Verna Fleming's legs. They are nice and slim, and there are a lot of leg men that would approve of them. But they are not for me. I need kachunga legs to get me going."

"To get you *going*?" I lifted an eyebrow at him.

He had the decency to blush. I use that phrase because just about this time I was reading a book by L. Sprague de Camp, I think it was, and the narrator in it said something very much like that.

I'll never forget one line from one of his novels, in which an ant-like humanoid is crawling out a prison window from which the bars have been half broken. He says something like, "These fertilizing bars have disembowelled me." I don't think I liked humour much in my science fiction then, but I do now. That's why I read Spider Robinson. And I can't forget that bit of ant-man monologue, though I can't remember whether he was wearing anything.

"I mean," said Will, "kachunga legs arouse my interest as no other legs can hope to do."

"How is that pronounced, again?"

"Ka-CHUNG-a!"

"From the force behind your syllables, I would guess that these chuglunka legs are powerful, perhaps even superhumanly so?"

"Ka-CHUNG-a!"

"These legs are, what, muscular?"

"Muscular and a little frightening," he said, his eyes wide open.

"Could you describe them? Give me a couple of examples?"

"Well, it's not that the ankles are bigger than usual compared with the rest of the legs. I know that's what you like, Cap'n."

"One of the variations I like. I also like slightly too muscular calves."

"Yes, well, that's not the way kachunga legs work. Let me try to put it this way —"

"I don't want to see you put it any way," I couldn't help saying.

"You misunderstand me, sir. Probably intentionally."

"Objection noted. Please proceed. Give me the specs for a pair of grabuncha legs." I closed my copy of Donovan's *Brain*, with a dandelion stem bookmark, signifying that Will would now get even more of my attention.

"Kachunga legs," he said, patiently and almost studiously, "are such that every part is to every other part in the proportions that you will find in the legs approved by critics as perfectly comely. That is to say, and never mind any stupid puns about my observations, if the perfect thigh has, say, 2.55 times the diameter of the perfect ankle, and I am just supposing these numbers, that arithmetic will also apply to the kachunga leg."

"Is that all you want to apply to the unpronounceable leg?"

"I will come, never mind, to that later. The kachunga leg, in a nutshell, is firm, strong, muscular, slightly frightful, and irresistible when flexed between a white bobby sock and a somehow lifted Stuart plaid skirt."

"And what does one imagine, because I have an intuition that that is your main focus here, doing with a kachunga leg?"

Will's face, which over the course of the years I had seen go from childish to adolescent, was as innocent as that of a Holstein calf. He took a deep breath, and sighed as he released it.

"Don't laugh. I imagine pressing every part of it, to my cheeks."

"You'll shave first?"

Unlike me with my baby-bum cheeks, Will had been shaving since he turned fourteen. Now he blushed a little, and I surprised myself by flinching a bit.

"That would depend. Would she rather have a smooth cheek, or a bit of razor burn?"

"Who?"

"Whoever the lucky woman was who had these kachunga legs."

"Not piano legs."

"No, definitely no. Kachunga legs are curvaceous and just like regularly beautiful legs, only more commodious."

"I am not interested in toilet fantasies, Trump."

"What are you talking about? I didn't say anything about a commode. We are perhaps in her bedroom, the window open to the verandah, breeze coming through the peach trees. I have my cheek against one kachunga leg, and then I turn my head and kiss it. Pretty soon I am licking this wonderful leg."

His eyes were closed. He was blushing right down to his shirt collar.

"Go on," I said, interested despite myself.

"I want these wonderful and powerful legs around my waist, around my shoulders, around my neck. I will go to heaven wrapped in these kachunga legs."

"You could be a demented genius, young man. Much more of this and I will find myself getting hot about, say, kachunga arms."

"There's no such thing," said Will Trump.

I reached into my shirt pocket and pulled out my Professor Dandelion spectacles, round frames with no glass, and put them on, adopting a look of aged wisdom. I had on one occasion been thrown out of the classroom for tomfoolery with these specs. Now the teachers just ignored them.

"I admit to a low grade of curiosity about these storied legs," I said, my chin in the fingers of my right hand. "Can you provide some examples?"

"No girl in my class really owns a pair. No one in yours does, either, though Pauline Knippleberg might be said to be on the way there."

"So where do you see them? I don't imagine that there is a magazine devoted to photographs and stories about the gathunker leg."

"I know that by now you are doing that on purpose, and if I did not have faith in the never-ending running joke I would tell you off."

"Apology accepted."

"And I can tell you one example that will illustrate my quest."

"You can't illustrate a quest."

"Miss Verge."

Now I felt *myself* blushing to my shirt collar.

"*Those* are the legs you've been slobbering about?"

"Oh, Merciful Minerva, yes! I have spent hours of my teen years thinking about those legs of Miss Verge's."

"And while you were thinking about them, were you also —"

"Oh, yes."

CHAPTER 21

I HAVE MENTIONED that I was the official scorekeeper and sportswriter for the OBCS baseball games, but did I also mention that I did the same thing for the Southern Okanagan High School basketball team? Our school colours were green and gold, and I guess there was a lesson there — that yellow gets called gold if you are thinking of your image. The team was called the Green Hornets after a contest to name it. The contest was won by a gink who knew nothing about sports, as far as I could tell, a grasshopper of a guy with straw hair from the British crowd. The Green Hornet was a comic book and radio hero, and I congratulated myself for my elite taste in deploring the theft of his name for a school's sports teams. In later years I would curl my lip when I saw famous comic strip characters like Snoopy and Bart whatsisname being used in badly-rendered imitations to promote school dances or garage sales. When I wrote my basketball stories for the Oliver *Chronicle* and the Penticton *Herald*, I always referred to our team as the Hornets.

It might have been the same kid, or another kid from the same litter, who won the contest to name Oliver's annual summer holiday. Penticton to our north had their Peach Festival. Osoyoos to our south had their Cherry Festival. This kid won with the dopey designation Apricot Fundae. Oh, please, I said, when I read the result in the *Chronicle*.

Maybe a long way deep down inside I wished that I could be a basketball player instead of the scorekeeper. But being a score-keeper and especially a reporter was kind of satisfactory in that it was an indication of my intellectual prowess. I loved knowing more about basketball than the players I covered. I also knew that the guys on the team would not have a clue who Isaac Asimov was, and would have a little difficulty handling the subjunctive.

"Were I you, I should practise my Cousy-like ball-sharing," I would say to one of our guards.

"The fuck are you talking about, Retard," would be his reply.

I did manage to make it onto our volleyball team, but a lot of that might have been due to the fact that I had made it past six feet tall, and most of the tall guys were on the basketball team. Volleyball was not a big game at sohs and the other Valley schools. The basketball team filled the stands at the school gym, but we played volleyball mainly at early hours in front of a few noisy junior high kids.

A few years later, when I did make it onto my air force station's basketball team, my coach would say I should pay less attention to looking photogenic and more attention to fighting my way to the basket, however ugly it might look.

I wanted to look good as an ace reporter too. I had found a green fedora in a storage room at the community hall behind the right field fence at the ball park, and adopted it as my signature topper. Sometimes I reshaped it to make it look like the pork-pie hat that my hero Lester Young wore. At the *Chronicle* I got the printer to make me up a pile of little cards with the word PRESS on them. I tucked one on an angle into the hatband and then tipped the fedora back on my head. I looked just like a reporter in a Superman comic strip. I knew that in real life no reporter had such a simple word on a card in his hatband, just as I knew that bank robbers did not flee while holding bags with dollar signs on them. But being unlike other kids involved humour as much as it did good grammar. That summer my little brother found my pile of PRESS cards and handed them out to passing grownups.

Wit and wisdom was a phrase I used to hear. I thought that they were pretty well the same thing.

Whatever they were, they were pretty well the things that separated me from the athletes I was annotating and writing about. On reflection all these decades later, I realize that my situation was not all that unusual. It was unusual in the area of Oliver, BC in the middle of the twentieth century, but not all that unusual if you looked around the continent. Almost all my life I have had conversations with intellectuals who are lifelong baseball fans. Basketball and boxing too, I guess, but mainly baseball. These are guys who write novels or teach history or draw political cartoons. These are guys who read Nietzsche. But they are proud to tell you Johnny Pesky's lifetime batting average (.307), and his real last name (you could look it up). They are all amused by the fact that they waste their time and brains on the physical exploits of guys who mostly got someone else to do their homework in high school.

Old ginks like me are particularly pleased when they hear about a baseball player who actually reads books or goes to an art gallery instead of a strip joint on the road. We are especially pleased by Miguel Batista, who has pitched for several major league baseball teams, and at age thirty-seven is a starter for the Seattle Mariners, at the time of this commentary. He is not only a reader, but Batista has *published* a book of poems and a novel.

Regrettably, most professional athletes are more interested in collecting vintage automobiles and diamond jewelry than books. When the US Olympic basketball team appeared for games in Athens, a malicious reporter asked their huge centre whether they had been to the Parthenon. This worthy replied that he couldn't remember the names of the clubs they had been to.

In my own mind I thought of myself as kind of interesting, walking into the gymnasium with my scorebook and a pocketful of pens. But I was, all right, a smart ass. Well, I thought at the time, what is the use of being smart if you are not going to be a smart ass?

Especially in the dressing room. Who could not be a smart ass in the dressing room? I was the kind of lad who was too shy to look at other guys' peckers, and I sure didn't make any jokes about peckers and so on. So I don't remember what the hell I might have said to Mickey Morgan (not his real name) that evening before the Keremeos game. Maybe it wasn't something I said to him in particular. Mickey was about six feet seven inches and way over two hundred pounds. Maybe it was just some general remark about the possible inverse relationship between brains and muscles.

Well, what happened was that on his way out to the court Mickey gave me a shot, something like a rabbit punch, a sucker punch, a chop with the edge of his hand to the back of my neck. It was a famous and seldom-seen fighting manoeuvre, maybe from jiu jitsu, which was notorious at the time. For the second time in my school days I was knocked unconscious. The first had happened in grade four, when I missed a kick at the soccer ball and fell backward onto the round rocks sticking out of the dirt of the boys' playground.

When I came to this time, I was dizzy for a while. I felt as if my upper vertebrae had been knocked out of alignment. But I was as noble and romantic as ever. I did not take the opportunity to deduct two points or add one foul to Mickey Morgan's line that night. Who won the game? Probably we did.

*A*T ABOUT THE same time that winter I carried my smart-ass
skill to the stage, or at least the rehearsal stage. There I went
after that asshole George Delsing. I knew I wouldn't have to
worry about a sucker punch or any other kind of punch from
that bozo. Delsing was another teacher's kid, his old man being
the physics instructor. He walked around school trying to look
mysterious and fatal. One day all his clothes would be green
and he would have a meerschaum pipe in his mouth. Next day
there would be dried blood on his forehead till mid-afternoon. He
would write poems in India ink on lined foolscap and leave them
on desks and tables. Terrible poems. All about headhunters in
Malacca and so on. Guys who killed their brothers with household appliances. He fancied himself a cartoonist as well. He'd
do piss-poor caricatures of teachers and monitors and leave *them*
on the tack boards. He carried a Baby Brownie camera like mine,
and snapped pictures of the sky. I hated sharing a first name with
this gink. I was afraid, I guess, that the name wasn't the only
thing. But I did not then, and I do not now, go in for psychoana-
lyzing myself and others.

It happened that we were rehearsing for Oscar Wilde's *The Importance of Being Earnest*. I didn't think then how peculiar it was to have teenagers playing turn of the century British fops, but I was impressed quite a bit that we were performing something by a really important writer instead of things such as *Muggsy's Merry Christmas*, which Will Trump and I had romped through the year before.

I am going to assume that you know the story that unfolds in *The Importance of Being Earnest*. If I ever see the movie on old-time TV now, I can mouth most of the lines, Delsing's and mine. He played John Worthing, and I was his foppish friend Algernon Moncrieff. Oh, I say. "I don't play accurately — anyone can play accurately — but I play with wonderful expression."

Around the stage it was a little harder to hang onto my sense of intellectual superiority than it was around the basketball court. Most of the young actors were pretty smart, and certainly hep when it came to arty-farty stuff. I did like to think that I was a bit ahead of Delsing, though I had to hand it to him — he did know who Dizzy Gillespie was; he did know about Vincent van Gogh. A year ahead of us had been Clayton Perry, the best actor I had ever seen up close. I admired him and suspected that he was at least as smart as I. And he was more daring than I — once, when he had forgotten a line, and the prompter did not whisper it loud enough, he stepped over to her hiding place behind the edge of the curtain and stentoriously asked for the line. I wished that I had such nerve.

So now that Clayton Perry was gone to the Coast, to university, maybe, though he came from a Sawmill Road family, Delsing and I were after his place as the star. I hope you understand that I am saying that word with a touch of sarcasm. It was with sarcasm that I went to work on Delsing. During rehearsals I would imitate all his tricks — if he half-whispered a line and looked off into the space above the audience area, I would half-whisper my reply, and look as if I were trying to see what he had been looking at up there. If he took up a manly pose with one foot in front of the other, I would stand the same way. If he blew a line, I would invent one. Sometimes, knowing how hard it was for him to remember his lines, I would slip him a sentence I had made up on the spot. He would be stuck for a response, and the prompter and then the director, Miss Farnholm of the adequate breasts, would talk to us with a voice just barely held below yelling.

Not satisfied with mimicking him during our Wilde witticisms, I went after him in the wings, in the dressing room and through the halls of dear old sohs. If he squinted his eyes and pouted his lower lip in what he thought was an interesting way, I would get behind him and do the same thing. If he affected what he thought was a deep south accent, I would reply as if I had just graduated from a nineteenth-century Prussian military academy. If he took a picture of a tree trunk, I would snap a photo of my knee.

It seemed to take him forever to catch on. I don't think he got it till the day that Wendy slapped the top of my head for aping his look, a turned up shirt collar and a slouch, hands in back pockets.

He smiled with his mouth closed.

So did I.

Wendy whacked me again.

Next day she whacked me three times, and at last Delsing seemed to twig to what was going on. It was then that he started planning his revenge. I had no fear that he would deliver a rabbit punch with the edge of his hand. That would diminish him in his own eyes. He had to think of something witty and secretive, something that would, if anyone figured it out, contribute to his reputation as a youth both intelligent and romantic. Well, if not romantic, at least picturesque in his invisibility. It took a week for his plan to hatch.

Seeing as to how I was an intrepid sports reporter for the Penticton *Herald* and the Oliver *Chronicle*, and thus a paid journalist, I did not think I should lower myself to writing for the high school paper, a typewritten and mimeographed organ called *The Scroll*. I did allow myself to lend my words to the SOHS annual, even though I disapproved its awkward name, *The Okana-quen*, and I wrote material for the noontime radio show Will and I did on the PA system, but I was not going to write for the badly-produced and teacher-approved monthly. If it had been rolled up as its name suggested, I might have thought of it.

But the February edition of *The Scroll* purported to feature a short poem by one "George Bowering," an atrocious bit of crud that threatened, as I saw it, to slow the ascent of any writing career I might seek to achieve. I was not yet thinking of myself as a writer — writing was something I just naturally did, a normal result of reading, one of the ways to show that I was not going to be a cherry picker or an auto mechanic in the future.

I didn't save anything in those days, so I don't have my old baseball stories in the *Chronicle*, and I certainly don't have the "George Bowering" poem sent to *The Scroll* by George Delsing, that dip. I don't have the letters that Wendy sent me a couple years later when I was in the air force. I don't have the cards I made from Shredded Wheat separators and traced comic strip faces. I don't have the Bremerton Braves baseball uniform I was given for helping around when the Wenatchee Chiefs did their spring training in Oliver, but that's because my mother chucked it out after I left home, though I thought of the house as my storage unit.

Here I am, putting things off.

I will give you my best impression of some kind of memory of the poem in question.

Oh mistresse fair, my eager soul's true aim,
Oh, chestless girl, who dandles my poor heart;
I long for you tho' erst for looming fame,
And comes the latter, surely we must part.

Though eyebrows do not grace thy brownish eyes,
And ankles thick do end thy shortish legs,
In swim suit under Okanagan skies,
You mimic bacon and two poachèd eggs.

Oh Celia sweet, come injure me with hugs,
And kiss me where I cannot grow a beard;
Prepare a couch where there will be no bugs,
And show me love is bad as I had feared.

My hipless wonder, set a gourmet's table,
Or take me out to dinner in the stable.

I don't know whether the teachers caught the duplicitous *entendres* in this scurrilous hack's composition. I am pretty sure that I didn't. But I was properly embarrassed.

I think I would rather have had another rabbit punch.

⊂━⊃

IF YOU HAVE managed to read or skim this far, you will know that things happen or don't happen to me in threes. Mickey's rabbit punch was scary because I had blacked out. Delsing's poem was embarrassing because I could never persuade anyone that I didn't write it, and more than that, there were parts of it that seemed familiar. I almost felt as if I could have written it. It sounded like a guy who is inwardly noble and romantic and uses tough humour to disguise that fact. But I would happily have accepted the cowardly blow and the snide plagiarism if I had never found Wendy's letter.

You remember how the beloved's handwriting could put goosebumps on your heart? You remember that I often roamed the brown rocky hills up behind the elementary school, with or without my dog Dinky? Usually I had a drugstore paperback novel in my back pocket, sometimes a magazine. I have a photo that Will took of me up in the hills. I am wearing my Georgie Hat and reading a copy of *Hit Parader*. My Georgie Hat was not to be confused with my reporter hat. My Georgie Hat was also a fedora, probably found in the cloakroom of the community hall, but it had the front brim turned up and pinned to the crown. Sometimes the back brim, too. In the cooler months I would have a scarf tied over the top and around my chin. Now I remember that the other lyrics magazine was *Song Hits*. You can't believe how thrilling it was when these mags arrived in Frank's pool hall in Oliver. I pretty well knew all the lyrics of all the hit tunes, which used to amaze my friend Roy Collett, who wound up playing bass in his own cocktail jazz trio ten years later, but these wonderful mags, made and sold cheap by the Charlton company, along with its lesser-known comic books, connected me with the shiny two-bit world of the eastern US, where I almost felt that I belonged. Like most US magazines, the November 1951 issue of *Hit Parader* reached small-town Okanagan news racks in September 1951.

This one likely had the lyrics for Tony Bennett's "Because of You" and the Four Aces's "Tell Me Why," with Al Albert bending the note on "me" and making sure there was a lot of light on his teeth for the group photo, while the rhythm section kept the doo-dum doo-dum going behind him.

"I keep fooling my heart."

I have probably figured this narrative all out by now, or if I haven't, I shouldn't be allowed to write this memoir, or at least to pretend that I am capable of analysis in its composition, as they say.

I mean, how did the letter get there?

And how come I was the one that found it?

I guess that at the time I thought that my hiking alone in these hills was a fully private and lonesome activity, known to me and my Creator. I will not, as some might do, peg Him as the one who arranged for my finding the letter. But there is a sliver of my brain that leaves room for that exigency.

To fold back again, just for a bit, I'll say that I don't right now remember whether I told you about that frozen guy and the fingers, but I think I did. The climber guy they found dead when the snow melted?

Okay, there was another step in the maybe true maybe not true story. Supposedly, before I met her and got to love being with her, Wendy had been this guy's girlfriend for a while. Now you have to remember that Wendy was a grade ahead of me in school, but a year and a month younger.

I could not ask her.

Especially when the story hinted a little further, (and where did I get this, did I imagine it or did I hear it whispered from a friend or enemy?) that Wendy had gone all the way with this romantic doomed young man.

It seems silly now, because it is easy to think back and do the arithmetic. If Wendy had gone all the way with him it would have happened a year or so back, and back then she would have been barely into her teenage years. Nowadays it would seem at least possible, but not then, at least not with an intelligent and wholesome daughter of the Anglican Church and the English community that ran orchards south of Oliver in the fifties.

Anyway, I don't think there was any question that Wendy's letter was addressed to that guy. Which only makes it worse, I guess, though I thought: what if this is a fake? But then I knew Wendy's handwriting as well as I knew anyone's, or almost as well as I knew my father's, say, or mine. No, it had to be her handwriting. In pale blue ink on an even paler blue letter paper. Under a rock on top of a larger rock in my favourite little cave in Cryhat Valley, where Will and I used to eat our oranges and practise cowboy dialogue.

So someone had put it there, in all likelihood someone who was watching me even as I went into the little cave and lifted the smaller rock. Someone who apparently didn't much like me, or who maybe just liked the opportunity to bother the ears off someone who thinks he is alone in his hike or his daydream.

When I first unfolded the light blue paper and saw the handwriting and saw that it was a letter, I assumed that it was addressed to me, that this was an elaborate gesture of affection. But I soon saw that though someone meant me to read it, the letter was addressed to someone else. Unless Wendy herself was at the helm of the ruse — which was an eventuality I did not want to entertain then, and which I don't much like to consider now.

I would or would not like to reproduce the letter here. But it has disappeared. Maybe I balled it up and threw it over a cliff. Maybe I burned it. Maybe I put it on the ground and pissed on it. I know that it is not among my papers at the National Library, which do contain letters I wish I had never got. Well, it wasn't addressed to me, so it wouldn't have gone there anyway. You will notice that I am putting this off. Okay, I can not, for whatever reason, present it here in its original shape. Suffice it to say that I was hurt as only a teenaged boy on a mountain can be hurt.

Funny verb, that, now that I come to remember the first time I heard it. It was from Wendy herself, sometime over the preceding year. I don't want you to be hurt, she said, I think. And I wondered about that: does it mean hurt feelings? But it sounded more serious than that, more intimate. But then I got to thinking about the word intimate, which always made me think of inside the brassiere.

Okay, the letter. It was not addressed to anyone, or rather, there was no salutation at the beginning. But it said this and that, in Wendy's handwriting, in Parker's blue ink. I will not say much more, except that it referred to "you," whoever that was, being inside her. My girl.

Now that I think about it, the person who put this little blue folded paper under that rock was probably watching me open and read it, watching from behind a rock, with field glasses. Smiling. I can't see a face. I never thought till this moment — maybe a female person?

No, female persons did not hike around these hills. I never ran across any. But who knew about my favourite cave? Will did, but he was out of the question. Maybe he told someone. Not likely.

Anyway, this letter, I did not know this then, but I grew to know it, or maybe to admit it, this letter was worse than getting judo chopped or misrepresented in doggerel.

I imagined my beloved naked that night and in many nights to follow, but now in my imagination she was no longer alone.

I HAD AN agreement with Will that he guaranteed to eat any sandwich I made him, as long as the ingredients came from the Bowering family's kitchen refrigerator, a Norge, or cupboards in the same room. He did pretty well, too, though he went slowly on the one that featured tuna and Scotch mints. On the Saturday after my arranged discovery of Wendy's letter in the cave, we were having sandwiches at the kitchen table, on this occasion joined by our ex-British pal Nigel Lamb, who for the occasion was dressed entirely in a Boy Scout uniform, though he was not a member of the Boy Scouts. He was also equipped with his usual monocle, which he placed in either eye as the whim took him. Also present was our Osoyoos pal Joe Makse, who had accompanied his mother to St. Martin's Hospital, where she was to stay for a few days. The hospital was only a block from my place, and Joe was staying with us for the weekend.

In addition to eating gourmet sandwiches we were drinking cups of the potato champagne my parents had been trying to make. I have no idea whether any fermentation had taken place, but we put on a show anyway, making extravagant gestures with our mugs, holding sandwiches aloft.

"Today's subject," I said, "is love." I took a sip. "Love has left me with a sore heart, but I remain her adherent. Call me foolish, but I revere love above all other emotions we mortals display."

Will had wrinkles in his young forehead. He would have come up with a reply, but I continued before he could construct his first sentence.

"For a youth, there can be nothing greater than a true lover and a true love. The fortune of birth, the possession of wealth, the quest for honours, are mighty things in themselves, but none of them can inspire a guy the way love can. Sure, it is a big drag to feel ashamed in front of your parents or your classmates, but that's nothing compared to disgrace in the eyes of your girl if you really love her, eh? You'd rather die than desert her."

"I don't know, George," started Nigel, but I wasn't finished.

"Love is the only thing that can make you die for someone. Your mother or your sweetheart, or your best friend, say."

Will gave me the white-eye and leaned his head in the other direction.

"So it's love, eh? Nothing approaches it."

I turned to my sandwich, as if the subject had been dealt with. But oh no, along came Will Trump with a discrimination.

"I would have to agree with you, Cap'n, except for one problem," he said, slowly and studiously. "The problem is that there's more than one kind of love, my friends. As a person who lives the life of the mind, I feel that I must recall for you, had it slipped from your memory, that there is the kind of intellectual and spiritual love that I tend to experience, and then there is the kind of banal physical attraction often called love by those who have a less-finely tuned consciousness."

Nigel put his drink and his once-bitten sandwich on the pale yellow Formica tabletop. He narrowed his already narrow eyes to put on the appearance of thought. His monocle fell onto his sandwich.

"I believe that you are distinguishing between true love and a kind of animal lust often misidentified as love," he said, as if to a witness in a stand.

"Not at all," retorted Will, my best friend. "I will agree that it is honourable to love a scrag such as Bedelia Glotenschnaubel, a love that is free from base acquisitiveness, and that it is also fair in love as in war to resort to devices that might on the face of it appear less honourable, as long as the desire is pure."

"You don't know what the hell you are talking about, Trump," said Joe.

"Very likely true," said that worthy. "But I can tell you this: it is not the experience of being in love that makes a difference; it is the manner in which one pursues the prize. Vulgar love is without value, but spiritual love is eternal."

"What about getting your oil changed?" enquired Nigel. "What about dipping one's wick?"

(Readers will understand that these were four innocents conversing on this Saturday noon in a small town kitchen. Notwithstanding my experiences with Miss Verge, of course.)

"My point," said young Trump, "is that you can achieve your greatest desire without being crude about it, that going all the way can happen naturally in a spiritually coloured love pursuit."

Swallowing a mouthful of white bread, peanut butter, hotdog relish, mustard pickle and shaved baking chocolate, I entered the lists.

"I believe that Will Trump, in his ham-handed way, has blundered onto the path that could lead to wisdom, had he the sensibility to travel it."

"Oh yeah? Well up yours with a ten-foot pole," were the words this person addressed my way.

"What I, blessed by innate intelligence and lucky experience, contend is that love, the more elevated love championed by my constantly eating satrap, will command all the more worthy behaviours. It will bring peace to quarrelsome people, quiet repose to the anxious, good will to those who vie with one another in business or sports or parking lots —"

"This is Oliver. We don't have any parking lots," put in Will.

"Love, in short, heals all troubles and fills the air with music."

"Then how come all those cowboy songs are always complaining about being mistreated by the guy's girlfriend, or the wife's husband?" asked Joe.

"He's got you there, Cap'n."

I stood, went to the cupboard on the left of the sink, and came back to the table with graham wafers, as if they were what I had intended to find.

"All right," I said. "If you three do not mind, I will proceed in another fashion. Do you mind if I ask you a few questions, thus leading you toward an intelligent regard for the actual nature of love, our topic for today?"

"Was that the first question?" asked Nigel, practising his usual weasel expression.

"I will ignore that oft-repeated attempt at wit," I said. "The first question is mounted thus —"

"Mounted! Tee-hee!"

"Herewith the first question."

"Lay-on, MacDuff."

"Lay! Tee-hee."

I counted to five inside my head. The silence seemed to serve the reacquiring of the deference I deserved.

"I believe that we often tacitly agree on a kind of personification of love. Perhaps a god of love. Perhaps a kind of ideal personage we call Love. Am I right?"

"Right," said one of us.

"Okay. I was going to go somewhere with that, but now I think I'll try something else."

"This is that other fashion you decided to proceed in?"

"Dialogue. I call it dialogue. It will show a great respect for your inquiring intellect."

Nigel leaned forward in his chair and produced an explosive fart.

"Very good," I said. "I see that you are pushing your brain to its limit. Now. Can we say that in love we desire that which we do not have, that we do not possess the object of desire? For if we desired it we would have no use for desire?"

"Use for desire?"

"You know what I mean," I said, not the best bit of logical argument I had ever proffered while sober, which was always.

"We use desire?"

"Close enough."

"Proceed with your questions, my elder."

"But once you no longer lack something, is it fair to say that you no longer desire?"

"Certainly," said Will, placing two graham wafers into his mouth, and tipping some failed potato champagne into there as well.

"So if love is a desire for something you lack, does that mean that you love beauty only if you are without beauty yourself?"

"Wait. Slow down," is what Will would have said if his mouth were not jammed with graham wafers and raisins and the like.

"That is if you already possess beauty, you have to desire something ugly?"

"Bedelia Glotenschnaubel," said Nigel, a light bulb over his head.

"Say," said Will, after swallowing as much as he could. "Does that explain why Wendy lets you hang out with her? She's sort of three-quarters good-looking, and you can manage one-quarter on a dark night."

"I just hope," I said, "that the philosophical lesson I tried to impart to you whippersnappers will do you some good some day when you are not expecting such a thing. Now I have a decree to make."

"What?"

"It's a new kind of sandwich called a decree. This will be my third," I said.

If it had been a movie, they would have thrown food at me.

BEFORE I TELL you about my next talk with Jeanette MacArthur, I guess that I have to confess about Mrs. Wilkins. Mrs. Wilkins recently passed away at a greatly advanced age, after two years of sharing a lunch and dinner table with my mother at the assisted living place under the hill across the river from downtown Oliver. Mrs. Wilkins had become Mrs. Worth some years ago. When she lived next door to us she was the mother of Darryl and Carol Wilkins. It was Carol Wilkins who gave me my first broken nose in a failed game of statues. It was Darryl Wilkins who always wanted to be the bad guy in our gun battles, and who later had a big collection of shirts and worked in sales or something in Edmonton. Later his mother became the step-mother of Ron Worth, a guy in my class who much later went into real estate sales in Oliver after being somewhere at the coast with IBM or some other place with initials.

You will notice that I am delaying this, putting it off, daw-dling, not quite ready to admit to being a peeping Tom.

The Wilkinses lived on the corner of two streets that may have had names down at the village hall map room, but had no signs telling us what they were, and in truth, nobody really knew, though I had heard somewhere that the street in front of our house may have been 6th Street or 6th Avenue. Anyway, we lived one house in from the corner, and my little bedroom was in the southwest corner of the house, though it had no window looking south at the street. The Wilkinses' bedroom was in the southeast corner of their house, and, I don't know, maybe twelve feet or so from my room.

Looking back now, I find it hard to believe that I was peeking out the window every night after lights out. Part of the problem was that my kid brother had his crib bed in my room when he was about two and I was thirteen. Another part of the problem was that after lights out I was usually reading a western novel or baseball magazine with a flashlight under the covers. I had no idea that most of the writers I would get to know would tell me that they'd done that too. Anyway, I may have suppressed a bunch of memory here, or I may have experienced swings of boy Christian puritanism.

But I do remember one memorable night when it was dark out, and I had my light out, and Mrs. Wilkins did not have her light out, and she also did not have her curtains drawn.

I think that Mrs. Wilkins may have spoiled me for the rest of my life when it came to what a woman's tits were supposed to look like. First she was walking back and forth in her bedroom, with her white brassiere on, a powerful looking brassiere, because her breasts were big and pointed and just wonderful for a young teenaged boy to see. She disappeared from sight and then reappeared, walking, touching her hair, picking up a brush and touching it a little. Once she put her encased breasts in the palms of her hands and pointed them at the mirror on her dresser.

"Oh please oh please," I whispered.

242 • GEORGE BOWERING

She reached behind her, elbows up, shoulders forward a little. "Oh please," I whispered. "I won't ask to see anything else."

And there they were! When the brassiere fell from them and was pitched somewhere, they hung for a moment, and then when Mrs. Wilkins straightened her back they rose and rose. They were white, with nice large dark brown nipples. I almost looked away, it was so wonderful, this sight I hoped I would see often in my life.

She put her hands under them again and lifted them a little, pushed them against one another, making a beautiful line between them. What would I do, I wondered. I hated Mr. Wilkins, an overweight Hawaiian-shirt-wearing guy with a glistening smile. What would I put there, could I kiss her, Mrs. Wilkins, I mean on her big lipstick mouth?

Mrs. Wilkins put her finger and thumb in her mouth and then squeezed a nipple. She actually smiled. Holy Moses, I wonder all these years later, did she know or imagine that this skinny boy was looking at her from his forlorn window? She smiled, Mrs. Wilkins, and gave them just a little shake. I didn't want to see anything else, maybe her bum a little, but that was all. Then she slowly pulled the curtain closed.

I went to bed and continued my visit with Mrs. Wilkins.

⸻

YES, THAT NIGHT I did not read under the covers. I don't recall what book I was reading that day and the next, but there is a good chance that it was a western.

In my reading of westerns, I didn't know it, but I was rehearsing a contradiction that would share my head for the rest of my reading and writing life. I have always been a little bothered by that contradiction, but also glad that I experience it in its many forms. But then I think no, a contradiction just suggests that there are two qualifications, whereas there ought to be dozens. Then I lose track of my thoughts and just feel my brain surveying what we have right here and kind of enjoying it. If that is too vague or seems not worth following, I agree with you, but there it is.

(Okay, if you don't want to think about this, just skip to the part about my next meeting with Jeanette, in Chapter 24).

So for example, during the times when I have lived back east I have been a strong advocate of the west. Living in Quebec I would complain that not all the news worth reading is about Quebec politics, that there are interesting stories on the west coast too. But when I am living out here on the west coast and hear people complaining that they don't want to hear about Quebec separatism, I elevate my sparse eyebrows and tell them that they should get their heads out of the Pacific Ocean and pay attention to the manifestations and elections in Quebec.

"Shut up, Bowering," they say.

"*Mange la merde*," I suggest.

Or about writing and publishing. My agent, who snuck half a dozen books of mine into the Penguin Books list, has got used to my lifetime love affair with the little literary presses with their miniscule and questionable readership. When I show a weird little manuscript to her, or just describe an idea from the dark side, she says, "That'll have to be one for your small press friends. Come back when you have a good idea for a non-fiction best seller. Get back on the A-List, dope."

So when I am reclined in some cluttered little firetrap above a laneway in the heart of ethnic Toronto, say, some of my oldest friends look at me funny if that is the week some "professional" press has published my novel and got it reviewed in *The Globe and Mail*. It's okay. I do feel guilty. I know that the most interesting poems and stories in the country are being published by fugitives from the visible world. I know that guys almost my age have eaten Velveeta sandwiches so they can get my chapbooks of acerbic verses into the hands of the forty people who want to read them while sitting and waiting for the prune juice to work — and that in a few years rare book store ginks will be offering them for sale for fifty times what some lovely subscriber laid out for them.

But I always wanted to get known. Not famous, not totally famous, because if you are totally famous you have probably got by without too much working out of the brain cells, and without an overdose of scruples. Or maybe I just assuage my own conscience from time to time, as when some glitzy magazine offers me hundreds of dollars for a couple poems they can stack between the Hugo Boss ads, and I say no, my friends, my real friends are never published in such magazines, and don't even read them. And neither do I.

This clears the desk that is my conscience, and I can then sign the contract my agent has sent me, in triplicate. I almost made it through life without an agent, but she found me, thank goodness, oh shame, whew. I didn't have an agent for the longest time. Was it because I didn't want to go all swell and betray my small press sweethearts, or because I was too stupid mixed with too shy to figure out how to get an agent, which would indicate to any loiterers that I didn't have one, and how come, when all the latest graduates from the UBC creative writhing [stet] department have them?

Anyway, maybe you get the idea. Now here is the way that contradiction showed up when I was fifteen years old and reading hundreds of westerns. I have mentioned some of the books I read during this unremarkable adolescence, but I have not said much about them. In later years, when I mentioned westerns, people took it for granted that I was talking about movies, which, part of the time, I was, especially, for example *The Tall T* and other oaters made by Budd Boetticher, though at the time I wasn't aware of his name. Anyway, I don't think I was, not yet.

All right, all right. The contradiction, if that is what you would call it. And if you think that we're here departing the main theme of this book, you haven't been paying close enough attention — not that I blame you. Okay, in those days I always said that my favourite western writer was Max Brand. I especially liked the Silvertip novels. Silvertip was a lone rider with a white patch in his hair. He had a very special horse and a wolf who accompanied him on his adventures. He was, as I would later figure out, a direct descendant of those heroic knights with their special steeds and special weapons who battled ogres and evil knights in Scotland centuries before. Silvertip was noble and romantic, just like me. He could do the seemingly impossible. He could swear an oath. He was a force for retribution or redemption in an old west that resembled a moon. I loved it. It was just about Biblical. It would prepare me for Borges. Miracles were not to be confused with miracles, but nearly, if you see what I mean. If you don't, read Luke Short.

Luke Short was on the other side of my contradiction. His characters were not endowed with any special gift or opportunity. They depended on their skill, and there was never any question of hoping for a suspension of the laws of physics. Luke Short showed you guys with sweat in their hats and whiskers on their faces. In a Luke Short novel there was no shooting guns out of hands. It was more likely that someone would get his hand shot off — by someone behind him. Or while he was sleeping. In a Luke Short novel, the old west was about water rights and hard digging in gold mines.

So I was a sucker for realism, too. A few years later it gave me an inner thrill to see the names of the tunes in the jukebox in a book by a Black USAmerican novelist depicting the streets of a city I had never visited. I was right there. The arm of God did not strike people down — the teeth of capitalism did.

I liked them both, Max Brand and Luke Short. I have no idea whether they liked each other. I think I liked Max Brand better. I always told myself that. But realism was attractive too. It took you away from your family romance.

Max Brand wrote under a lot of different names, and I read as many of his books as I could get hold of, except for the Doctor Kildare ones. I would leave those for the readers who would later turn easily to television. His real name was Frederick Faust, and he wrote hundreds of books. Just before D-Day in 1944, four years before I started reading him, he was hit by German shrapnel while sitting on a kitchen chair on a hillside in Italy, and died, fifty-two years old. Fifty-two would always be my unlucky number. There's nothing rational there.

Luke Short was the name of an actual historical (as they say) old west gunslinger and gambler. No one knows for sure whether the writer who chose that name knew about the gunslinger, but I have to believe that he did. His birth name was Frederick, too, Frederick Glidden, but like his opposite, he chose a name made of two one-syllable words that sounded inherently western. He didn't die in a chair. He died nearly blind in Aspen, Colorado in 1975, trying to see details.

⌒

YOU THINK THAT this stuff isn't the kind of colourful narrative you expect to see in fiction, or in a memoir like this?

Well, look.

A bullet came through the book the reader was fitfully reading, and pierced the hard bone of his forehead.

CHAPTER 24

J EANETTE AND I got our casts off at just about the same time. We arrived in school on Wednesday with shrivelled white arms and bits of guck between our fingers. I could be heard yelling "ow!" every time I bumped my newborn arm against a doorjamb or some other innocent woodwork. Jeanette must have been banging her arm against things too, but we never heard a sound from her. Bob Fleming the math teacher even gave up the chance to get off a few wisecracks. I spent the whole first day taking furtive sniffs of my uncovered arm, trying to capture the last bits of the wonderful smell. My mother had shown me how to wash carefully with warm water and a sponge that morning, ruining a great opportunity. During the four classes I was in with Jeanette, I kept my eye on her, but she didn't raise her arm to her nose even once.

I had a study period just before the bell that afternoon, and my plan was to sneak out early, pleading lavatory business, to make sure that I would be at the bridge before Jeanette could get there. But Joe Makse and I got into this routine where we had to write down the names of all the one hundred and twenty-six players in the National Hockey League, and the final bell rang a few minutes before we remembered Pete Babando. I had to hightail it across the rocky ground from SOHS to the little ditch.

But there she was, just reaching the bridge, stopping a second to shift the books held against her secret chest, obviously trying to favour her bad arm. It crossed my mind that she had gone deliberately slowly from locker to door to bridge. Nah, I told myself. Well, maybe.

But she was not about to say anything to start a conversation. In fact, she looked at me for maybe a half-second before she hitched her books a bit and started walking down the hill beside Fairview Road's old ragged pavement. I was carrying only one book, and not a schoolbook, because as usual I had finished all my homework in all my various classrooms throughout the day. I could have offered to carry her books for her. The book I was carrying was just a drugstore paperback — Frederic Brown's *What Mad Universe* — but I was afraid that if I offered to tote her books for her, I would be the recipient of some powerful school-girl sarcasm.

She was wearing the kind of clothes a teenaged girl shouldn't have to wear, but she acted as if she didn't care, and maybe she didn't. I know that even though we were living in a hick town, there were guys who had all the right clothes, and I wished that I had them too, often settling for something less even if it was in the right direction — well, actually, if it was in the right direction and it was less, that was the worst thing possible. I knew that, but what could I do? The guys were wearing those drapes, and chains that looped down beside the right pocket. Ross Fitzpatrick, who would grow up to be a senator, had a gold chain made out of the letters of his name. As for me, I got the chain off a bathtub plug and worked something as best I could. Pathetic.

I could pretend that I didn't care. I did have some wine-coloured drapes, from the Eaton's catalogue.

But did she care, or was she aware, or what? I couldn't figure her out. In her cheap plaid skirt and cotton shirt that looked an awful lot like a boy's shirt, she looked — nice. Could have been pretty, and maybe she was, but she did not have a bit of cosmetic colour anywhere on her face. Her eyebrows were a little bushy and uneven. Her bobby socks didn't have enough elastic in them. But her eyes, hazel eyes with shards of yellow in them, glistened when she suddenly stopped looking down or away, glistened with some kind of unknowable pain that looked like pure beauty, not a kid's beauty, but a grown woman's knowledge that could be transmitted only as beauty.

And if that sounds too much like amateur poetry, screw you!

"I can smell your arm from here," said Jeanette.

"Lucky girl!"

"If I was your mother, I would wash your arm and then I would wash your mouth out with soap."

I felt a leap of affection in my chest. I didn't know it, but I had been looking for a girl who would say things like that, quickly. She could be Catwoman to my Batman. Or what if I were a wise-cracking superhero named Smart Alec? She could be my Alice.

"If you were my mother I would do all my chores without arguing," I said, wondering whether I was winning or losing this match.

We walked for a while, her head down looking for nickels, maybe, my head up, checking for a change in the weather.

"I think if I were your mother," she said as we crossed the highway, looking in both directions for safety, tucking our weak arms under our ribs, "I'd run away from home."

"Alice one, Alec zero," I said.

"What?"

"I am just putting in aimless dialogue here," I said.

We turned the corner at the angled street that led to Sawmill Road. I tried to slow our pace. She seemed to be trying to speed it up.

"I know how you got your arm broken," she said.

"Fell off a plank into a hole," I said, lifting my chin. "Can I sniff your arm?"

She showed me her arm. There was a fist at the end of it. She must have been a tough girl. I couldn't clench my fist yet.

"I know how you got your arm broken," she said. "And there was no plank and no hole. You just made those details up from some other experience."

"I am interested in how you got *your* arm broken," I said, a little nervously.

We walked for a while. She dropped one of her books once, and got between me and it before I could bend and fetch it for her. She did not bend her knees and squat to pick it up as the good girls were taught to do. When she bent over to get it I saw the backs of her bare legs. If only I had not decided that our relationship would be based on human sympathy and noble intentions, I might have imagined what a teenaged boy imagines, or imagines that he imagines. I had seen her breasts for two seconds, after all.

"Maybe I fell off that plank of yours into that hole of yours."

She was clearly not going to discuss her arm and the breaking of it. When I had taken a picture of her with her cast, which she had tried to hide before the shutter nabbed it, and developed and printed that picture under Will's basement steps, and tried to give her a copy, she had given me a glimpse of the fire in that place behind her eyes and walked briskly away.

"What mad universe," I said, but didn't know why.

"O brave new world," she said. We had been taking *The Tempest* in English.

"East of the sun and west of the moon," I said.

"I did it."

"What? Did what?"

"I busted your arm. Broke."

"Hardy har har," was my incisive reply.

"It was me."

"I."

"Me."

"All right. I give up trying to help you with your English grammar. I will switch my attention to refining your logic and memory and so on. You could not possibly have done it. How did you do it, for example?"

"Example?"

That was to demonstrate to me that I did not hold all the high cards in the composition of English.

"All right. How did you, a mere slip of a girl, break my arm?"

There I had her. We had stopped walking, and now faced each other on the gravel edge of Sawmill Road, what would be a block from her little house in the toolies, if there were blocks down here.

"No, I did not do it literally," she said, "but I am responsible. You are, too, I guess. You were in the wrong place. You were trespassing. Anyone would know what you were up to out there in the dark."

What, I asked myself, did she think I was a peeping Tom? A simple peeping Tom? She thought I was trying to catch a glimpse of her skin? I didn't think that that was her message when she flashed her breasts. I thought it was something more complicated, something about vulnerability and poverty and other abstract words I was always unable to sound. A peeping Tom? All right, with Mrs. Wilkins I was a peeping Tom. Maybe with

Winnie and Polly I was a kind of orchard peeping Tom. But there in the reeds beside the river?

Now Jeanette was not looking down at the dry ground, not glancing away, not avoiding my eyes. She was looking straight at my eyes, looking a little upward so that I should have been able to catch sight of that fire moving inside her. But I saw no fire. There were tears filling her eyes and falling down her cheeks. There were no makeup smears, only those unexpectable, incomprehensible tears.

⁓

WHEN I GOT home no one else was there. I filled the woodbox and the sawdust hoppers, then I put all my books in alphabetical order, then I took the keys and walked to the post office and brought back the mail, then I looked at all the pictures and cartoons in the new issue of *Sport* magazine that was my share of the mail, then I actually went outside and pulled a gourd off the vine that had edged its way under the fence and into the alley. Then I sat down in the kitchen and wrote a poem about Jeanette and her eyes. I dropped it into the wood stove. I wrote another one, in which I said noble and romantic things about a girl's eyes. Luckily, it too went into the stove, and to make sure that no one else would ever see it I even scratched a kitchen match and set them both on fire. Then I wrote a poem about that dead horse I had found two summers ago, and this poem I kept for several months before I burnt it.

Those eyes full of tears and brave poverty were the last I ever saw of Jeanette MacArthur, the one I did not understand. She was not at school the next day, and not there the day after that, not there on Monday. On Tuesday I got up early and sort of ran all the way down to her house with the intent of maybe walking her to school, as if we were friends or going steady, or I was her bodyguard. But the place looked empty. I don't know how, but it looked as if it was empty, and there was no truck around. I even went and knocked at the front door. The wood sounded puffy.

She was gone in the middle of the school year. Who could understand such a thing? She wasn't the first classmate to be gone in the middle of the year, but I felt terrible. Who could I ask about this? I was a schoolboy with a C+ average. Could I go up to the principal's office and ask where Jeanette MacArthur was?

It felt awful, as if she had died, like Tibor Palley, only worse, because I had been trying to — what? Save her? There was something awful, and I could not do anything about it, and worse than that, I didn't have any idea what it was I could not do anything about.

I did not try to write any poems about it, that's for sure. Except for one.

 ❧

THAT NIGHT I took the long mirror off the bathroom door and put it on the floor, and stood over it looking down. I could not tell whether what I was looking at was scary because it was so low or because it was so high. I could not decide what I was doing with a mirror on the floor.

CHAPTER 25

I HAD TOLD myself not to get anywhere near Miss Verge again, but for some reason I kept finding more reasons to go to The Hub pool hall, the one we called Frank's. Sometimes I went the two steps down into the cool pool room with the lights over the tables that left the rest of the area in darkness, not expecting to get into a game, because I was officially underage, though I did play there once in a while when there wasn't much business and I had a friend with me against whom I had a chance, as I never would have had against, say, Ritchie Schneider.

The point being that The Hub was two doors away from The Food Basket, above which Miss Verge had her apartment with the hardwood floors and the beaded curtain. I must have told myself, as I was walking slowly past her sidewalk door, that I was giving myself up to chance — if she happened to see me, okay — if not, I'd go and leaf through the *Police Gazette* at The Hub. There were a lot of good sports stories in the *Police Gazette*, especially about boxing, but it wasn't strictly a sports magazine, so I didn't buy it. It also had a lot of stories about guys getting the electric chair, and, let's face it, pictures of strippers and b-girls in what folks called scanty outfits. I would stand at the magazine rack and read as many paragraphs about, say, Sugar Ray Robinson as I could before Frank said something. He tended to be easy with me, because I bought a lot of baseball magazines and western novels at his establishment. I liked the smell in there. I couldn't help looking at pictures of scantily clad strippers, could I?

So when I came out into the Saturday sunshine I could hardly see, and I had a bit of disturbance inside my brown corduroy drapes. I stood in front of Frank's for a while, trying to get my eyes and my pants back into shape. Remember, the main street in Oliver is Highway 97, and on Saturdays all the orchard families from north and south came into town to do their weekly shopping and socializing. The street was packed with cars, parked cars and slowly cruising cars. Cars and pickup trucks. There were parents and kids all over the sidewalks and taking crooked paths between the slow cars to the other side of the street.

I knew that Wendy and her parents would be in town sometime during the day. It was a warm November, and for the first time in seven months there was no panic situation in the orchards. The cold storage rooms at the packing houses were full of apples, and sprinkler pipes were stacked beside tractor sheds. Seasonal pickers were gone to whatever jobs they did in the winter months. Winnie and Polly were back in Grand Forks or Castlegar, wherever their Doukhobor colony was.

I loitered in front of The Food Basket, and saw Freddy Jones in there, filling brown paper bags with groceries. I waved at him, but he just looked past me, toward the freedom of Saturday. A Saturday in November made me a little nervous. The orchards were full of trees with nothing but leaves on them, and the packing houses had cut back to skeleton crews made up of men and women who had worked there for years and years. It was strange not to have a job. I could be home splitting firewood and ripping out the remains of the summer garden, two chores I actually enjoyed. I couldn't hang out with Will because he was counting inventory at his father's machine shop, or as Unca Ted called it now, The Plant.

Now there I was, loitering in front of the door that separated The Food Basket from Tuck's Cafe, looking at the passing show, my green fedora over one eyebrow. I was carrying a copy of *The Last Space Ship* by Murray Leinster. I read Murray Leinster because he was a prominent science fiction writer whose books appeared in drugstore paperbacks in a little town in the British Columbia interior, but he was not my favourite. He was kind of like the Luke Short of science fiction, a guy who liked to get all the scientific and engineering details right. He was big on space ships and how they worked, and never one to go off on flights of fancy.

So there I was in front of that door on the main drag on a warm Saturday afternoon, holding a science fiction novel in my hand. In that way I was a departure from the norm. Usually on a Saturday afternoon there would be a guy in a cheap suit there, holding up copies of *Awake* and *The Watchtower*. I never saw anyone buying a copy of *Awake* or *The Watchtower*. I once saw a guy there holding a copy of *Awake* in front of his chest, his eyes closed, looking asleep as a person could be while standing in a suit on the sidewalk. I once saw my sort-of cousin — I couldn't figure out whether we were related or not — I think he was the son of someone named Ruby, a woman who might have lived in a trailer with my mother's brother Amos, a guy who had broken every bone in his body except for his cranium. Anyway, my cousin or whatever he was, should have been back in the East Kootenays but here he was in Oliver one year, I don't know why, and he looked embarrassed there on the sidewalk in front of The Food Basket, as if his family were making him do this,

Jehovahs, people used to call them. They discouraged their kids from reading anything but *Awake* and *The Watchtower*. I was kind of afraid to read these things. The people selling them were always dressed up in cheap suits, even in the summer desert heat. I felt sad for my sort-of cousin and for all the people selling those weird pulpy magazines on the street.

But here I was in one of their spots. On a whim I stood up straight and held my copy of *The Last Space Ship* in front of my chest. I got a few looks from grownups, the kind I was used to getting.

Miss Verge closed her door with hardly any sound, and as she passed behind me, she whispered, "Meet me at the school."

"It's Saturday," I whispered, but she was too far away to hear me, probably. I waited for a while, watching her hiking up Fairview Road, then I took the street that would have passed our house if I hadn't taken a left at the first cross street.

I ambled. I didn't want to catch up to Miss Verge, and I didn't want to gather any attention by hurrying. She was going fast because she always did, and if anyone saw her they would think it was pretty normal, and she probably wanted to get there before I did anyway, to check it out.

"It's Saturday," I said inside my head twenty times and aloud about four. Oh, I thought, she probably wants me to help her move something, boxes of Home-Ec stuff, probably.

~

THE SCHOOL WAS a big E-shaped building, some kind of modern architecture, with a light yellow stucco surface, surrounded by fields of round post-glacier stones that bad boys had to wheelbarrow down to the bottom edge of the schoolyard. In later years there would be lawns here and there, and Phys-Ed soccer players got to play on grass instead of stones. When I was a kid I didn't know that soccer was played on grass in some parts of the world. There were guys in my classes who were from Displaced Persons families, but I never talked with them about soccer. I wanted to hear about being a kid in the war.

Now I tried the general access door next to the gym, which was a rectangle at the end of one of the E's arms or legs or whatever you would call them. The door was locked. I looked around, trying to be invisible. Then I went and tried the door next to the auditorium, which was a rectangle on one of the shoulders, I guess you would call them, of the E. It was locked as tight as a banker's heart. As invisible as I could get, I walked around the auditorium. There must have been twenty outside doors on that school, and I passed a few as I went toward the teachers' door — that is the door that would take you from their little stony parking lot to the hallway outside the principal's office.

"Europa!" I whispered as the thumb latch gave and the door was mine. Invisibly, I stepped inside and put my back to the wall.

Okay, I had found the open door. Now to find Miss Verge. What was I doing this for? I wasn't really a detective, just a secret hero.

"Doo de daw dee doo," I sang.

Sotto voce.

Because I was scared. All right. When this immense school was being built, Will and I were about eleven, and we used to explore the tangle of concrete rooms that would become the basement. Once we were in a dark room, and just outside the room was a guard or janitor of some sort, a guy whose flashlight never quite caught us.

"I see you in there," he shouted. "Come on out."

Will started to get up from his prone position, but I held him down.

"You idiot! They always say that," I told him, *sotto voce*. I was always instructing him in the ways of the spy in those days.

But I had been scared too, though I never told him, and if you are reading this now, Will, you finally know. So now, standing as invisible as possible with my back to the wall ten feet inside the teachers' door of sohs on a Saturday afternoon, I was scared in just about the same way. Then the janitor, not Joe Jackson but the other guy whose name I didn't know, came into sight. I stopped whispering my song.

I didn't know what I should do. It was not absolutely against the law for a student to be inside the fortress on a Saturday, but it was a little strange.

"Hi," I said, in a whisper, really.

The guy walked right by me, no more than six feet away from my visible standing body.

"I haven't seen you," he whispered, and went out the door. I heard the lock go ka-chunk.

It was quiet in the school now, quiet and dark and cool. I could smell floor wax. The little light I could see was coming in through the November windows and the big night lights that marked every seventy-five feet on the hallway ceiling. I strained my ear for Miss Verge. Then I started very slowly, trying to keep my shoes quiet, along the hallway to my left. I stopped in front of the door to the main office in front of the principal's office. Should the door have been closed, I wondered. It was open a little, and when I pushed two fingers at it, it opened wide, with just a slight creak.

I could have just gone home. The outside doors were locked but any of them would have opened from inside. I could have escaped. Well, I thought, I still could, any time I wanted to. But I felt my cock pressing just a little bit against my pants. So I stepped into the office. There was a counter with an open part, and a desk and a few chairs where bad boys would wait when they had been sent to the office for behaving imperfectly in class. Beyond this furniture was the door of the principal's office. That information was printed in black letters on the pebbled glass that made up the top half of the door. It was not light enough now to read those words, but I knew them well. For one thing, it was here that Will and I had run our noon-time PA radio show.

The door to the principal's office was open just a little.

I could have turned around and done my searching and exploring and general scaredy-cat shenanigans down the hall and to the right and down to the Industrial Arts rooms.

But I couldn't resist.

"I see you in there," I said, just a notch above *sotto voce*. "Come on out."

There was such a silence that I could swear I felt a tuft of breeze at the back of my neck. I stepped to the door and put my hand on the edge. My eyes were adjusted to the dim light in the outer office, but it was a little darker in there. I reasoned with myself that inside that room there could be a homicidal looney-bin escapee armed with a scythe. I pushed the door open further.

It was so quiet. I felt a run of goose-pimples up my hairless right arm. I remember that as if it was going to start happening right now while I search my memory bank for the moment.

I stepped into the room, holding my arms in front of me. Something must have told me not to grope for a light switch. My eyes were adjusting slowly, but there were mainly shadows in that room, shadows and a square blur of light that must have been the window with a curtain in front of it. In the South Okanagan any windows that faced south had to have curtains on them, to keep the desert sun from baking whatever it could reach through glass.

Close those curtains, my mother would say. We do not need a hothouse in here.

But I was not thinking of my mother in that darkened room.

My hands, which I had been swinging back and forth across my path, touched a lamp on a desk, and a second later I knew what I was touching. Still I did not try to switch it on.

I stood absolutely still, except for the blood that was speeding through my arteries, and held my breath. So I heard breathing that was not mine. It was behind me and to my right. I held my breath as long as I could, and when I let it go it was a loud burst of used air. I listened some more.

"Hold still."

There was no question about whose voice it was. I held still, and the next thing I knew the voice was next to my right ear, whispering. I could feel breath against my ear. Boy, I hope I am right, I told myself.

Now there was a shift. I don't know whether I heard it or felt it somehow or knew it with my lately developed extra sense. But I knew that she was right behind me, and close.

"Put your hands on your head."

What would you do? It was too late to run. I put my hands on my head.

"Do I get a last cigarette?" I asked, my voice a whisper and somewhat shaky.

"You don't talk during this," she said, and the whisper was right behind my back.

This? Oh boy, I said to myself. Will is never going to believe this. Well, he is not going to hear it from me. Not till we are old farts and Miss Verge is only a memory.

A small hand reached around under my upraised left arm and held the right side of my breast as if it were a tit. Then a small hand came around the other way and held the other one. My boy's nipples stuck out, as I had felt only when I stepped out of the lake into cool air. But it was not particularly cool there in Prune's dark office.

I felt her body, especially the part that was pressing against my bum. Then her hands moved.

"Shhh," she advised.

Her hands moved, opening button after button on my shirt. Then it was fully undone and her hands returned to my chest, playing with my nipples now. No one had ever done that before. I was surprised to know that such a thing could feel so good. But my arms were getting tired. I lowered them, and as I did, she deftly pulled my shirt off and let it fall to the dark floor.

"Hands on head," she said.

I put them up. My heart was pounding. Why couldn't I just walk on out of here, shirt be damned? But there was no chance of that. I imagined facing a panel of judges. There was nothing I could do, your lieges; she did not hesitate to use all her authority.

My belt. She had the slightest little trouble remembering which way it opened, but soon it was under control. Then the top button of the fly in my cords. Then lickity-split, the zipper. My cords plummeted to the principal's floor. There was a good-sized bulge in my jockey shorts, and even in the dim light I could see or imagine that the nose of my cock was showing where the lorn elastic could not quite contain it. Then she leaned harder against my bum while her right hand held the cotton-covered bulge. Now she was breathing, not in my ear, she being too short for that, but pretty loudly in the otherwise quiet air. I assumed, that is, that I was the only person who could hear the blood pounding in my temples.

Both arms were around me again, and both hands were at work. The left reached inside my underpants and held my aching cock while the other gently pulled my underpants away from my front and down my thighs. I heard a knee crack as she squatted and pulled the underpants right down to the floor. At a hand's signal I lifted my left foot and then my right, and I no longer had anything around my ankles. I was naked in the semi-dark except for my shoes and socks. That seemed strange but all right.

She was standing again, and now she had one hand under my balls and the other just holding my cock, and I just couldn't help it, there it went, into the semi-darkness in front of me somewhere, three gouts of it. Her hands caressed me as my cock went from up and swollen to almost down but still swollen. I felt a short, stocky, roundish, naked body against my back, and a squeeze, a teacherly squeeze, I reminded myself foolishly.

I would have done anything then, with no thought of going home, no fear for a moment of sudden principal door bang.

So when she spoke I did as I was told.

"Close your eyes."

Done.

"Turn around."

Done. I could feel cold sperm on my thigh.

"Open your eyes."

I did as I was told. And now that my eyes were adjusted to the room's dim light, I could see her. She was completely naked except for high-heeled shoes. Her body gleamed as best it could in the shadowy school air. Those large breasts, a boy's hot dream, were high and hard where you might expect them to droop from the sheer weight. The high-heeled shoes made her thighs look even more muscular than they were. Her curly hair stood out from her head, no schoolmarm, no, no Shorthand instructress, some girl grown out of a dark home into eyesight — I reached toward her, I don't know, breast, shoulder at least, just something, while I felt boyish in my naked skin, I needed some kind of touch to get past the post-ejaculation embarrassment.

I reached, and as I did she showed me what she had in her hand.

Two seconds went by, and then I knew what it was. We were

in the principal's office after all. I was being a bad boy after all. I had got the strap twice in my school years, once in grade four for punching a girl who had been kicking me and hitting me with a book, and another time in grade eight for a reason I can't remember and probably disputed at the time. The strap really did hurt, and though there were boys who were bound to get it from time to time, we all knew enough to keep quiet when someone like Sammy Kouzmanoff came back from the office with a face red down to his collar and eyes that were just starting to dry up — I mean Sammy, the toughest kid in grade seven.

I thought she was going to give me the strap. I mean that thing really did hurt. We didn't know where principals got their straps, but we thought they had something to do with sharpening the cutthroat razor at the barber shop.

My head was in a spin, my body felt a little stupid, having oxblood shoes on its feet, and for some reason my right hand went out in front of me, palm up. In a flash of memory I saw the principal hit himself on the thigh when I pulled my hand away before his first whack. I looked at the short, naked except for high-heeled shoes, Miss Verge, and prepared myself for my punishment. Punishment for what? Well, for this. I shouldn't be doing this.

But she did not whack my steady hand. Instead, she placed the handle of the principal's strap in it. Then she turned her dim gleaming back to me.

"I think —"

"This is not the time to think," she whispered with a little vehemence.

"What —?"

"You know what," she whispered.

"I'm supposed to —?"

"Yes, you are."

She held her breasts in her hands and braced her high heels.

I gave her a slight tap. She was a schoolteacher, after all. In this school. I gave her another little tap, across the middle of her back.

"That is not a feather," she said. "It is a strap. Strap me."

I liked the way the wooden handle fit into my hand. I gave her a little harder slap on the back, between her shoulders.

"Harder," she said. She put her hands on the principal's desk and leaned over a little. Her hair fell on all sides of her face.

So now it was nearly impossible to hit the plump place between her shoulders. I reached and smacked her on the small of the back.

"Harder," she said, and leaned even further over the desk, so that now I could not really whack her anywhere but on her nice big white bum. Maybe it was because of her bum that I really let loose. The first whack was loud, a slap that was just short of frightening.

She gasped, and her high heels moved a little. I slapped again, a little harder. I gave her a chance to tell me to stop. My heart was pounding. She stuck her ass out a little farther, and I used my whole body, the way you are supposed to do when you are swinging at a fastball.

Christ, this is the last time I will ever get into a situation like this, I told myself, but I flexed my knees and whacked her hard. Even in the dim light I could see that there were red welts on her white ass. She grunted with each whack, and then she cried out. Then she made another kind of sound, one I had heard from her once or twice before.

I saw my cock. It was dark and it was sticking out and up.

I acted without consideration. Naked in my shoes, I stepped behind Miss Verge and put my sore cock up against her.

She wriggled her large reddened bum, pushing back against

me, teetering a little on her high heels. I didn't know how to do this, I just hoped that it would work. But my thing did not find its own moist place, so eventually, ashamed, I held it in my right hand and poked around until it went in. Then in my shoes and nothing else, I fucked the Bookkeeping teacher. She asked me, I thought, to do it harder, and so I did, bending my knees and hurling myself at her.

I wondered whether I was going to ejaculate again. Sometimes I managed to do it twice when I was whacking off. I felt as if something good was going to happen. My belly or whatever it was slapped loudly against her ass.

And she was making that noise from her throat again. I bent over her and rested my whole thorax on her back. I felt as if I should have said some words, and maybe I would have, but how could I? I was going on sixteen and she could have been twice that, I figured. Instead of words, I let out something between a big breath and a groan.

While I was lying that way, on my front, my heavy cock came out of her. I did not want to stop, and so I was pleased when she reached under herself and took hold of it. She elevated it, until it was nosing an aperture. I stood up and pushed it forward, but it was not ready to go in, not into that one. I held it again and lowered it and put it into the warm moist place. Then Miss Verge said an imperative verb and an objective pronoun, and I hurried to do her bidding. I moved faster and faster and hit harder and harder, and I don't know where it came from, but it spurted out of me again, just as Miss Verge called the name of a figure from scripture.

*T*HE JANITOR GUY whose name I did not know was sitting
on the steps outside the teachers' door. At first the bright
autumn sun hit my face so hard that I could not see anything.
Then I could see the steps with the guy sitting on them. He was
looking the other way, at a paperback book, and there was cigarette smoke rising from him. I had to walk right by him or across
the pitiful grass our school was trying to grow into a lawn. I
walked carefully and quietly.

I stopped and looked over his shoulder. He gave no sign that
he thought I was there. He blew cigarette smoke at the open
pages of his book. I wanted to see what he was reading, but
what could I do? Take the book out of his hands and turn it over?
Kneel down in front of him and look at the cover? Ask him? I
could have made it up for this account I am slowly and reluctantly composing. I could have said that he was two-thirds of the
way through *Seven Slash Range* by Foster Bennett, not one of my
favourites, but a pretty good serviceable western.

"Hi," I said as I passed him on my way down the steps, because
I didn't want to be rude, I guess, or I didn't know what to do.

"You're invisible. I don't see you," he replied, and when I turned to look at him he was looking down at his drugstore paperback.

SO I TRAIPSED on home, where my sister greeted me with the strangest words.

"Your girlfriend called you on the phone."

I stared at her. I didn't know who she meant. I didn't know then whether she was capable of irony or even a kid's sarcasm.

"Who?" I asked.

"Oh, there's a lineup of them now?"

All right, something close to sarcasm.

She meant Wendy, of course. Still, that was odd, because we didn't telephone each other unless we were doing it to convey a message from our parents for some mealtime or the like. Telephones were for adults and emergencies in those days.

"Okay, thanks, Sal."

"Are you going to phone her?"

"Yeah, later."

And I went down to my half-assed basement room. First I lay on my back on my rumpled bed covers, hands behind my head, a young male, my ankles crossed, eyes open and looking through the joists above me at the universe. I would figure out life. But I could not resist the temptation. There was a shiny new drugstore paperback of *The Warriors of Day* by James Blish. I wasn't too crazy about James Blish. He went across the line into werewolves and such. Later he would write lots of books drawn from *Star Trek*, the television show about far planets with humanoids on them. But I fell asleep with a James Blish book open and face down on my chest.

PINBOY • 271

on sunday i went to the Anglican Church with Wendy and her family. It turned out that that was what she had been phoning me about. Wendy told me that St. Edward's was a low Anglican Church. In the high Anglican Church they swing incense. High Anglicans are the English who really didn't want to be separate from the Catholics all that much. But I was a kid from the United Church Sunday School. I thought that it was tending toward idolatry to kneel down on the little fold-down kneeler in front of you when it came time to pray. It took me a long time to remember when to do a quick bob of my head twice during the reciting of the creed. And somewhere in that creed the worshippers said something about being "catholic."

Still, I was with the girl I more or less thought I was going to marry, or I was going to get officially engaged to, and here we were in her church, and though it was full of those English snobs and imperialists I had so much trouble with, I was impressed — it all seemed so much more serious than the United Church. I was a conflicted small town Montague.

They asked me to come out to the orchard for dinner, which was the local word for lunch, but I begged off, saying that I had goofed off all day Saturday and had a lot of chores and homework to do. Then I went home and got into my old clothes and started working. I chopped a huge pile of kindling. I filled both sawdust hoppers to heaping. I went up and down the alley in back and picked up every piece of trash, bleached Sportsman packages, chunks of unrecognizable cloth, even some popsicle sticks. I yanked up all the weeds that had made it into mid-fall, pulling smaller and smaller weeds until I was grabbing single leaves. I went through the house gathering ashtrays and washed them in the kitchen sink.

My mother gave me a look.

I went downstairs and made my bed the way they showed

you at Air Cadet camp. I picked up all my books and magazines and put them in a new sequence on my shelves, except for the outsized ones, which I kept on a chair. The arms of the clock on the kitchen wall went around slowly.

Or else time stopped and then it started again or slowed down and crawled and staggered, and there was nothing I could do about it. It was the longest Sunday of a life that seemed so long to me at the time. I laugh, thinking of that now, because the last fifteen years have gone by without my noticing. I still remember the score of the first game of the 1948 World Series, but I can't tell you right off who won the World Series in 1999.

It was Sunday evening, so there was no great elaborate supper (which is what we called dinner in Oliver in those days) in our kitchen, just something like grilled cheese sandwiches on square white bread and salad, into which my mother put a number of vegetables cut into tiny pieces. And Campbell's tomato soup, which I still think of as the natural partner for grilled cheese sandwiches. I usually scarfed such food as if I were afraid that the big bad wolf would arrive and lay claim to it, but this Sunday night I sat with one elbow on the table, a real no-no in that house, my chin supported by the hand in question, my food still in the bowl and on the plate in front of me.

My mother gave me another look.

‿☞

MONDAY MORNING AT school I didn't know what to do. Part of me wanted to hike upstairs to the area around the Typing and Shorthand rooms and just have a look at Miss Verge. I wouldn't be capable of speech, but I might signify something with my eyes, for a second or two raised from their downward cast. I could walk slowly back and forth in the hall between my classes. We got seven minutes between classes, enough time for teachers to duck into the staff room and have half a cigarette, or for the kids to get to their lockers and look for scrawled messages. I could go up the stairs two steps at a time during every intermission, and have about one minute for my stroll, for my pacing.

But the other half of me, or as it turned out, about three-quarters of me, wanted to stay as far away from Miss Verge as it was possible to stay. Just imagining being in the same hallway as Miss Verge, I felt my face blush or flush, and I felt that if I lifted the tail of my shirt I would see a lot of red skin.

I did not see her until Wednesday. I had settled down a little. At home I reverted to the minimum chores. At school I was back to my normal self, yukking it up or scowling darkly by turns. Then as Will and I headed toward the principal's office to do our little noon-hour radio show on the PA, she emerged from that meaningful room, her head down, till she lifted her face, and there we were, both still walking slowly, our eyes seeing what we had not prepared ourselves to see, those other eyes. I think that I probably flushed or blushed even redder than before. Her hair was perfectly combed, but her cheeks were red and her eyes were just beginning to fill with tears.

⸙

SHE WAS GONE before the spring term had much more than started. At first she was just off the job. Then she was away, and gradually she was gone. I went to her downtown door and watched, pretending to be waiting for someone to shoot pool with, but she did not show. Miss Verge was never again an Oliver citizen. She was replaced at the school by a Valley woman who came out of retirement for a few months.

I was confused about whether I was supposed to feel guilt. Or shame. Whatever that was. The difference.

I NEVER SAW any tears in Wendy's eyes, her small green eyes with barely perceptible eyebrows, set in her elegant English best-friend bones. For the next three years she would be trying to break up with me, and I would feel her up a little more each time: because one, I thought I had it coming to me for not taking advantage of her on the couch; and two, because I thought that I might lose her if I didn't go a little further. But I still did not, you should pardon the expression, press the issue, because I did not want to make a mistake in the opposite direction, and also, I suppose, because I was chicken and still kind of Christian, and she was certainly not, it appeared, the kind of girl who was going to put her hand inside my pants. A few times I thought that she might be thinking about it, though that may have been wishful thinking.

But I was more comfortable complimenting her mother on her home-made mayonnaise, bringing in firewood for the kitchen range, singing "Stardust" and hearing the news that I had not reached the proper note completely, and generally being Henry Aldrich to her Corliss Archer. You can look those people up — I don't want to make that easier for anyone. I will say you'll find that I'm mixing Henry Aldrich with Dexter Franklin. The latter was never a philosopher and neither was the former, but I think I was. Not the kind that Wendy was interested in, it turns out.

Really, I didn't have time to be a philosopher. I was a sportswriter, a stage actor, a volleyball player, a photographer, a cartoonist, a tuba player, a choir member, and a poet. I wrote one more poem about Jeanette that I thought was destined for greatness, so I burned my only copy and ran the ashes down our kitchen sink. I wrote one entirely different poem about Miss Verge, or really about me with Miss Verge as the setting, and I knew that it was too humorous for the occasion, so I cut it into many small pieces and walked from our place down the hill to her door, dropping a tiny piece of paper at each step.

I wrote a lot of poems about Wendy, and I could not bring myself to get rid of them. I thought I'd found the way to my lifetime devotion. It took me years and years, but I did manage to lose most of them.

ABOUT THE
AUTHOR

George Bowering is one of the most influential and prolific authors in Canada. His work includes writing for the theatre, poetry, fiction, history, and literary criticism. The originality, relevance, and quality of his artistic talent have been recognized with numerous awards, honours, and nominations, including the Governor General's Literary Award for Poetry in 1969 (*Rocky Mountain Foot* and *Gangs of Kosmos*) and one for fiction in 1980 (*Burning Water*). He was named the first Parliamentary Poet Laureate, and made an officer of the Order of Canada and a member of the Order of British Columbia.

While at the University of British Columbia, Bowering and fellow students founded the journal-poetry newsletter *TISH*, which introduced the post-modernist movement in poetry to Canada. He also founded the literary journal *Imago* and was a contributing editor to the journal *Open Letter*. He has taught in Calgary, Berlin, Montreal, and for thirty years at Simon Fraser University, where he is now Professor Emeritus of English. He lives in Vancouver.